Mentoring

Mentoring

How to Find a Mentor and How to Become One

Bobb Biehl

AYLEN
PUBLISHING

P.O. Box 1999
Mt. Dora, Florida 32756

© 1996, 2005, 2007 by Bobb Biehl
All rights reserved
Printed in the United States of America
0-9708623-9-3
Published by
Aylen Publishing

P.O. Box 1999
Mt. Dora, FL 32756
Subject Heading: Mentoring/Counseling/Friendship

Unless otherwise noted, Scripture quotations are from the New American Standard Bible, © the Lockman Foundation, 1960, 1962, 1963, 1968, 1971, 1972, 1973, 1975, 1977; used by permission. Verses marked NKJV are from the New King James Version, copyright © 1979, 1980, 1982, Thomas Nelson, Inc., Publishers.

ISBN 0-9708623-9-3

Acknowledgments

Thank you…

Cheryl, for being my life mate.

Claude Robold, for your leadership in the mentoring dream, your significant contributions in the review of this manuscript, and for coming through in a last minute crunch.

Bill Needham, for your research assistance.

Sally Horn (Tape to Type), for your typing support under great time pressure.

Steven E. Olsen and Dr. Skip Lewis, for your valuable contribution to the bibliography sections of this book. Because of your input, readers of this book will have a valuable head start on further work on the subject of mentoring. Your thoughts were also very pivotal in my thinking at certain points in the writing process.

My mentors and my models. Some are still living, others are not, but each one believed in me, and wanted to see me do well. Thank you for helping me continue to grow (listed alphabetically).

John Adams	Ron Beshear	Bill Bullard
Rob Acker	Bob Biehl	Calvin Burgess
Dave Adams	Don Biehl	Pat Caruana
Justin Agoglia	J. Biehl	Dave Cavan
Kristian Agoglia	Jerry Biehl	George Caywood
Bill Anderson	Doug Birdsall	Paul Cedar
Randy Andrews	Nathan Birky	Ben Chillemi
Bob Andringa	Chuck Bolte	Henry Cloud
Bill Armstrong	Shawn Boskie	David Coleman
Jerry Bach	Marv Bowers	Paul Conway
Frank Banfill	Tom Bradford, Jr.	King Crow
Bruce Barbour	Pat Bradley	Jim Daly
Bob Batterbee	Spencer Brand	Dave Day
Allan Beeber	Norman Bridges	Devin Day
Richard Beach	Bill Bright	Howard Dayton
Denny Bellesi	Ren Broekhuizen	Jack DeBartolo
Dave Bellis	Kurt Bruner	Darryl DelHousaye
Tom Berhens	Ben Bull	Bill Dembereckyj

Larry DeWitt

Jim Dobson

Lee Donaldson

Leland Donaldson

Steve Douglass

Mike Downey

Peter Drucker

Bill Duell

Chris Duncan

Lee Eaton

Loren Eaton

Eddie Edwards

Bill Elliff

Ron Elmore

Ted Engstrom

Rick Ensrud

Norm Evans

Terry Fleck

Phil Foxwell

Robert Fraley

Jack French

Bill Frisby

Eric Garcia

David Genn

David Gibbons

Jose Gonzalez

Jim Green

Mike Green

Marty Grubbs

Ed Gruman

Os Guinness

Jim Hagelganz

Curtis Hale

Bob Hamby

David Harmon

Daryl Heald

Howie Hendrichs

J. M. Herr

Dave Hewett

John Hinkle

Don Hodel

David Horner

Bill Hossler

Brad Howard

Howie Hugo

Sterling Huston

Bill Hybels

Dennis James

Frank James

Robert Jeffress

Derric Johnson

Steve Johnson

John Kang

Marvin Kehler

Gray Keller

Brad Kierns

Joe Kimbel

Tim Kimmel

Dick Koeth

Mark Kohler

Dennis Kowal

Fred Kuehn

Steve Largent

Bob Larson

Glenn Lavy

Robert Lewis

Paul Lewis

Rick Lobs

Dan Lorbetski

Jordan Lorence

Tim Luberski

Chip MacGregor

Bill Maddux

Tom Mangham

Jack Markle

Ken Martin

John McAuley

Scott McBride

Gary McCaleb

Caz McCazlin

Josh McDowell

Bob McEwen

Ed McGlasson

Jerry McKinney

Mac McQuiston

Scott Melby

Mark Merrill

Mark Miller

Drew Miller

Tom Minnery

Bo Mitchell

Al Mohler

Tommy Moorman

John Moran

Ed Morgan

Maynard Munger

George Murray

Lloyd Murray

Shawn Murray

Paul Nelson

Roland Niednagle

Wayne Noaker

Ed Orr

Larry Osborne

Bryan Owens

Gary Palmer

Ted Parker

Larry Pate

Duane Pederson

Tony Perkins

Dick Peterson

Carson Pue	John Sorensen	Michael Visser
Dave Raney	Michael Spraggins	Chuck Wallington
Dennis Rainey	Rory Starks	Jim Warren
Dave Ray	Tom Stebbins	Tony Wauterlek
Steve Reed	Rob Stevenson	Paul Weaver
Bob Roberts	Allen Stout	Paul Weber
Joel Robertson	Jim Subers	Al Weiss
Claude Robold	Paul Swets	Bill Wellons
Adrian Rogers	Wayne Swindler	Ken Wendeling
Chuck Roper	Chuck Swindoll	Ed Wentz
Greg Ruegssegger	Takeshi Takazawa	Russell West
Mark Russell	Don Teasley	Jay West
James Ryle	Charles Thaxton	Willard Westblade
Tim Sambrano	Alan Thomas	John Wheeler
Verley Sangster	Larry Thompson	Bill White
Skip Scheonhals	Bob Thune	Joe White
Jens Schmidt	Bob Tiede	Luder Whitlock
Alan Sears	Lee Torrence	Frank Wilder
Ray Shank	Ed Trenner	Lee Wilhite
David Sharbutt	Steve Uhlmann	Jeremy Williams
David Shibley	Glen Urquhart	Sandy Willson
Ricky Skaggs	Tim VanRyn	Kevin Wilson
Don Sloat	Jeff Ventrella	Steve Wingfield
Dave Smith	Ralph Veerman	Darrell Winrich
Ray Smith	Danny Villanueva	Steve Woodworth
Chuck Smith, Jr.	Barney Visser	Chris Zikakis
Bob Smullin	Dan Visser	

And to all those I think of as protégés—thank you for the valuable lessons you have taught me, many of which are included on the pages of this book.

Contents

Introduction   xi

PART ONE—*One Way to Make a Significant Difference*
1. What Difference Does Mentoring Make?   3
2. Why Is Mentoring So Important?   9

PART TWO—THE *ABC's of Mentoring*
3. Mentoring Is...   19
4. Mentoring Is Not...   29
5. Twenty-one of the Most Frequently
   Asked Questions about Mentoring   45
6. Anyone Can Mentor, but Not Everyone Should   59
7. Warnings   65

PART THREE—THE *Primary Benefits of Having a Mentor*
8. A Head Start in the Workplace: Professional Benefits   75
9. Security on the Mountain of Life: Emotional Benefits   83
10. The Bridge into Adulthood: Developmental Benefits   91

PART FOUR—A *Protégé's Perspective*
11. What to Look for in a Mentor   105
12. Finding and Approaching a Mentor   113
13. How to Be a Great Protégé   117
14. Thanking Mentors   119
15. Honoring Mentors Who Are Already in Heaven   123

PART FIVE—A *Mentor's Perspective*
16. What to Look for in a Protégé   129
17. Finding and Approaching a Protégé   135
18. How to Be a Great Mentor   139
19. Special Instructions to Special Mentors   145

PART SIX—BIG-PICTURE *Implications*
20. Developing Leaders for the Next Century   155
21. A Desperate Need in the Church of the Future   165

PART SEVEN—THE *Future of Mentoring*
22. Consider Making Mentoring Your "Personal Dream"   185

PART EIGHT—ADDITIONAL *Resources to Maximize Your Mentoring Ability*
A. Bibliography of Mentoring Resources   199
B. Protégé "Getting to Know You" Questionnaire   212
C. Questions to Ask to Help Your Protégé Define Her or His Dream and a Practical Plan to Turn the Dream into Reality   222
D. Resources   225
E. Quick Wisdom   237
F. Bobb Biehl's Speaking Topics   239

Introduction

Why are you reading this book? If someone asked you to put your answer into one word, what would you say?

Relationship?

You may say, "In my life, I really want to form relationships that are more significant to me. I don't know how to relate to people as I'd like to. When I was a kid, I was always off by myself on the playground. Since then, I've had a struggle getting really close to anyone. When I die, I'm afraid most of the people at my funeral—if anyone shows up—will be looking at their watches, instead of weeping. I don't want that to happen. I need some deep, meaningful relationships."

Lifework?

You may say, "My relationships are fine, but I'm looking for a new dream. I'm looking for a ministry that fits me, a lifework to which I can commit myself. I've accomplished a lot. I'm successful at what I do. I have lots of friends. But I'm really looking for something that will require the best of my energy for the rest of my life. I'm not an evangelist. I'm not a good discipler. I want to find a ministry that fits me, a ministry that God has been preparing for me. I'm looking for a new passion, a dream I can believe in for a lifetime."

Significance?

You may say, "I'm looking for a sense of significance. I need something that will last not only this lifetime, but that will also make a difference for generations to come. I want my life to count. I want to make a major difference in the lives of others."

If you are reading this book for one of those three reasons, let me say to you that the relationship you have been looking for, the lifework you have been asking God to make clear to you, or the significance you've been dreaming of can be found in mentoring.

Confidence?

Perhaps you are reading this book for a different reason altogether. Maybe you're interested in mentoring but lack the confidence to begin. Many people struggle with confidence as mentors or confidence as protégés, especially those who are new to the mentoring process. This book was written to increase your mentoring confidence.

Confidence is a by-product of predictability. The more predictable a situation is, the more confident you will feel in it. For example, if you go to a party where you know most of the people, you can expect the people will be glad to see you and make you feel welcome. The situation is predictable, so you go to the party with a great deal of confidence. But if you are going to a party where you don't know anyone, you have no guarantees that the people will like you or accept you. You can't be sure they will take you in and make you feel at home. The situation is not predictable, so you will not approach that second party with the same degree of confidence.

My goal is to make the mentoring process as predictable as possible. When you approach a mentor or a protégé, I want you to know exactly what to do and say next. When next steps and results are predictable, you will be more confident in the mentoring process. If you run into problems or difficulties, you will have this book to help you figure out what to do next. You can always have a deep sense of mentoring confidence.

Do You Want to Find a Mentor or Become One?

Do you long for a relationship with a person who can give you perspective, wisdom, support, and access to people and resources? Do you long for someone to guide you as you grow into your full potential? If so, you are looking for a mentor!

Do you want to experience the satisfaction of significantly influencing the next generation? Do you desire to help others win in life? If so, you have the heart of a mentor!

When I speak on mentoring, I typically ask, "How many of you have come to learn how to find a mentor?" Then I ask, "How many have come to learn how to become one?" The response is consistently fifty-fifty. There are as many people interested in giving as in receiving in a mentoring relationship.

The fact that you are reading this book gives me great pleasure. You had hundreds of options as to how to spend the next few hours. You are reading this book at this very moment because you are ready to learn how to find a mentor or how to become one. In fact, you can do both at the same time. I hope you will.

My Assumptions About You

I am taking several things for granted about you as a reader. I am assuming that you:

- are a Christian
- want to find a mentor, become a mentor, or both
- have many questions about mentoring
- want proven, practical ways to increase your confidence in the mentoring process

If my assumptions are correct, you are reading the right book!

By the way, I have not made assumptions about whether you are a man or a woman. This book was written for anyone who is interested in mentoring—young and old, rich and poor, all races and all nationalities.

Mentoring Is My Passion!

Bob Buford is the former president of a successful television company, the founder of Leadership Network, and author of the book *Half Time*. Not long ago we were attending a seminar. During a break in the session, Bob asked me one of his "zinger" questions. "Bobb, what is your passion today?" Without a moment's hesitation I replied, "My passion is MENTORING!"

Mentoring *is* my passion. I see mentoring as the critical link in developing, protecting, and optimizing Christian leaders for the next century! I'm writing to help you see my mentoring dream and make it your own. I hope you will be mentoring people fifty years from now. Next week you may not remember my name, but I hope you will have found a mentor and a protégé. You will have formed a relational network that will add security, acceleration, and depth to your life.

Several years ago, I was returning to my home near Orlando, Florida, after finishing a consultation with the Fellowship Bible Church in Little Rock, Arkansas. It just so happened that one of my lifelong friends, Dr. Luder Whitlock, former president of The Reformed Theological Seminary and now president of Excelsis in Orlando, was returning from the Jackson, Mississippi, campus on the same connecting flight. After asking an accommodating lady if we might change seats, we were able to chat our way from Atlanta to Orlando.

We talked nonstop. We discussed the state of the world, the nation, the Christian church, education, the inner cities—just to name a few topics. At a brief lull in the conversation, Luder asked, "Bobb, if you had unlimited resources and you could do anything to make the most difference in the world, what would you do?"

As quickly as I had answered Bob Buford, I replied, "I know exactly what I would do. I would help every Christian person I meet gain a clear understanding of mentoring because I am convinced that mentoring is the most critical thing we can do today to prepare and protect the next generation of Christian leaders."

By now it should be clear that mentoring is not just a passing fancy with me. For years mentoring has been and, God giving me strength, will continue to be my PASSION!

Mentoring: How to Find a Mentor and How to Become One **Is a Practical Book**

This book is full of "tomorrow morning practical" help in the mentoring process, developed over years of experience. I have wrestled for years with questions like:

- Who asks whom?
- How does mentoring differ from discipleship?
- How do I get started in a mentoring relationship?
- How do I find a mentor?
- Am I ready to become a mentor?
- How do I find a protégé?

In this book, I will share time-proven answers to these questions and many more. I will tell you everything I know about mentoring—

everything I would teach you if I were one of your mentors.

The information can be roughly divided into three categories:

1. Instruction

Each chapter covers some of the basic ideas of the mentoring process.

2. Inspiration

I asked people around the country to write tributes to their mentors. These tributes will inspire you to continue growing in the mentoring process. As you read the tributes, you will begin to see, in vivid personal colors, how life shaping mentoring has been to some of the finest leaders of our generation. It is my prayer, that at the end of your life, your protégés will say the same kinds of things about you, partly because of the time we have spent together in this book.

3. Information

The appendices describe additional resources available on the subject of mentoring. They will help you know where to go from here in the mentoring process.

Bottom Line

- I assume you are a Christian who wants to find a mentor, become one, or both.
- Mentoring is my passion!
- This book contains the practical ideas I would teach you about mentoring if I were one of your mentors.

PART ONE

One Way to Make a Significant Difference

As a young person, did you have a feeling of destiny?

Did you dream of growing up and accomplishing something of major significance?

Are you pleased with your progress on that dream to date?

Is mentoring possibly the key to making the difference you want to make in life?

CHAPTER 1

What Difference Does Mentoring Make?

Let me take you back in time. Remember when you were twenty-one years old (if you aren't twenty-one yet, go back five years). Remember how you felt: shy, arrogant, brash, insecure, over-confident, unsure, questioning. Remember where you were.

Now, remember the three adults in your life that you respected most and with whom you had some type of relationship. They knew your name. They would say, "Hi, how are you doing?" You weren't necessarily close, but you looked up to them and admired them a great deal. Take a moment to identify three adults such as I've described. Remember them?

Write their names here:

1. _____

2. _____

3. _____

Let's say one afternoon one of the three adults you looked up to called and asked you to go have a cup of coffee. Imagine that once you got past the small talk this highly respected person said something like this: "I know a lot of young people, and you are one of the most outstanding. I have been praying about it, and I would like to become one of your life mentors.

"What I mean by 'life mentor' is very simple. I want to be one of the people, whether you become the president of the United States or a prisoner, who cares whether you live or die and wants to see you win for the rest of your life. I want to help you any way I can. I want to put you on my lifelong prayer list, and when you have children, I want to know when they arrive, even if I'm living two thousand miles away. If you run into problems or just need a friend to talk to, I'll be available any time, day or night. I want to stay in contact with you no matter where you go or what you do for the rest of your life. I want to be one of your life mentors. Whenever we get together in the future, this year or in thirty years, I will ask you two simple questions:

- 'What are your priorities?'
- 'How can I help?'"

What difference would it have made in your life if even one of those three adults you listed had come to you and offered you a mentoring relationship like that and then followed through on his/her intentions?

> Stop reading for a few minutes and seriously try to imagine what difference it would have made.

Mentoring Makes "All the Difference in the World!"

When I've asked others that question in a one-on-one setting, the most common response I get is a slightly teary, "It would have made all the difference in the world!" Perhaps you have had adults like these in your life. If so, your response could very well be, "It made all the difference in the world!"

Now I'd like to ask you the flip side of this question. "Who are the three most outstanding, up-and-coming young persons you know?" They may attend your church, be members of your club, work in your office. These are three young leaders about whom you say, "That person could be head coach someday. That person could be chief surgeon someday. That person could be president someday."

Write their names here:

1. _____

2. _____

3. _____

At this point these young people look up to you. You get the feeling they like you. Whenever you pay any attention to them, they "light up." They respect you. But are they going to come up to you and tell you how much they admire you and ask you to be their mentor? When you were their age, did you tell the adults you looked up to that you admired them? Did you ask them to be your mentor?

Probably not! You probably watched, admired, and respected them from a distance. In your heart you hoped they would take the initiative by approaching you. Well, these three less-experienced people you consider future leaders are probably looking at you, and in their hearts, saying, "I sure wish I could get some time with that person!"

Mentoring begins by going to those young people and saying, "I'd like to be one of your life mentors, and what I mean by that is simple. I want to put you on my lifelong prayer list. Whether you become a prisoner in a federal penitentiary or president of the United States, I want you to know that as long as I walk the face of the earth, you have someone who is praying for you and wants to see you win. I want to help you any way I can."

What difference would it make in those young leaders' lives? If I asked them, I'm sure they'd say, "It would make all the difference in the world!"

Let me tell you a true story about George Caywood. At the time the following conversation took place, George was the president of the one hundred-year-old Union Rescue Mission in downtown Los Angeles,

California—a ministry with a ten-million-dollar budget and a one-hundred-fifty person staff.

When George was fifteen, he and his family attended church regularly. Life was not easy; he experienced the typical ups and downs of teenage life. One day George came home from school to discover his father had given up life's race. George's dad had committed suicide, and he had done it with George's gun. George had to become the man of the house, whether he wanted to or not, as a fifteen-year-old boy.

Years later, George and I happened to be in Washington, D.C., at the same time, so we decided to meet for lunch. We were talking about mentoring, and I said, "George, tell me something. When you were fifteen, what difference would it have made if one of the men in your church had come up to you, put his arm around you, and said, 'You know, George, there is no way on the face of the earth that I can even begin to understand what you are feeling right now. I haven't lost my daddy, but I want you to know that I believe in you, George. You're a good kid. You're going to make it. I'm going to pray for you for the rest of my life, no matter where you go or what you do. Just keep me up-to-date so I can know how to pray for you. Whatever you choose to become in life, I want to be one of your life mentors, one of your lifelong friends.'"

By this time, the tears, guided by sun creases, were dripping off George's chin. I asked, "George, what difference would it have made in your life today if that had happened when you were fifteen?" His mouth quivered as he said, "All the difference in the world. It would have made all the difference in the world!"

I ask many Christian leaders, "What difference would it have made in your life if someone had come to you, when you were twenty-one, offered to be your mentor, and followed through on the offer?" The response is almost always accompanied by tears, and it almost always comes in the same words: "It would have made all the difference in the world!"

While writing this book, I sent a letter to approximately one hundred people inviting them to submit a tribute to their mentors. I was amazed at how many people did not respond. In fact, I decided to call a few and ask, "Did you get my letter? Are you planning to write a tribute?" The most frequent response I received was, "I have never had a mentor."

Many leaders in our generation have never had a mentor. Others have, and for most of them having a mentor made a significant difference.

Ron Jensen is the president of High Ground Associates in San Diego, California. I've known Ron for over twenty years. One day he shared with me one of the most convincing accounts I have ever heard of the difference mentoring makes in the life of a Christian leader.

While finishing his doctoral studies, Ron personally interviewed the pastors of one hundred of the largest churches in the country. What he discovered amazes me. He found that the one common denominator among these megachurch senior pastors was that each of them had at least one mentor.

During the heat of difficult situations, many young leaders decide each day—in some situations, many times each day—whether to quit or to keep going.
Frequently, a single "cup of coffee" conversation is the watershed point in a person's decision-making process.
Is mentoring worth a few minutes of your life?

What Difference Can Mentoring Make?
"All the Difference in the World!"

"Attach a boy to a good man, and he seldom goes wrong," James Dobson wrote in *Parenting Isn't for Cowards.*

Bottom Line

Mentoring makes "all the difference in the world" personally and professionally!

CHAPTER 2

Why is Mentoring So Important?

By now you know that I believe mentoring is vitally important. In this chapter I want to show you why mentoring is so important. I can do that best by describing:

- why mentoring has been so important historically
- why mentoring is so important today
- why mentoring will be so important for our children and our grandchildren
- why mentoring will be important at the end of your life

Why Mentoring Has Been So Important Historically

I am proud to say that Dr. Ted Engstrom, president emeritas of World Vision International, has been one of my life mentors. I am also very pleased to say that each time I have had the opportunity to sit and chat with Gordon MacDonald, it has been a rich growth experience for me.

Dr. Ted Engstrom's book *The Fine Art of Mentoring,*[1] first published in 1989, contains a foreword by Gordon MacDonald that captures the essential reasons mentoring was important in the past and is even more important today. This passage is so rich, I want to quote almost all of it.

[1] *out of print*

I have a hunch that a book on mentoring would not have been necessary one hundred years ago, and an eighteenth century publisher might have muttered irreverently, "What's the fuss all about?" That's because, up until recently, mentoring—the development of a person—was a way of life between the generations. It was to human relationships what breathing is to the body. Mentoring was assumed, expected, and, therefore, almost unnoticed because of its commonness in human experience.

In the past, mentoring happened everywhere. On the farm, a boy or a girl was mentored along side of mothers, fathers, and extended family members. From the earliest years, these mentors gave children a sense of "maleness" and "femaleness" and taught them what work was all about and how it was done, what character meant, and what were the duties and obligations of each member of the community.

Mentoring was the chief learning method in the society of artisans where an apprentice spent years at the side of the craftsman learning not only the mechanics of a function, but the "way of life" that surrounded it. A similar pattern was pursued in the old university where a student learned in the home of the scholar: it occurred in the old royal court where the knight imparted the warrior's skills to the novice and in the studio where the artist poured himself into the formation of his protégés. In the world of spiritual development, the mentoring pattern was universal. Eighteenth century New England pastor and wife, Jonathan and Sarah Edwards, usually had one or more "disciples" living in their home where there was ample time for the learner to observe the quality of a marriage, personal spiritual dynamics, and the vigorous pursuit of pastoral activity.

In contrast to the past, the mentoring function today is in short supply. It is certainly not found in those homes where children part company with their parents for the better part of each day and accumulate an average of only eight to eleven minutes of parent-child conversation before the sun sets. And it is not found on most campuses where faculty and students rarely meet outside the class room. Nor is it found in many parts of industry where the craftsman has given ground to the technician. If mentoring has survived, you'll see it best in the world of athletics and the arts where outstanding performance can only be developed through individual, one-on-one encounters.

Today, what passes for people development happens in a class room, and the certification of a person is by diploma from an institution rather than the stamp of approval from an overseer, a mentor. The criteria for the judgment of people usually rests upon knowledge rather than wisdom, achievement rather than character, and profit rather than creativity. And as long as that is true, mentoring will likely be a second class matter in our value system.

But the good news is that more than a few are waking up to the fact that we have lost something precious in our culture because the mentoring function has been permitted to lapse into semi-obsolescence. There is a renewal of reference to mentoring in the business literature, the world of education, and in social work. And that new alertness has been in evidence of course in the Christ-following community also. Some are newly discovering that virtually all training of the people of the Bible happened in the mentoring context. Others are learning that preaching and acquisition of biblical knowledge is not enough to develop the sort of Christ-likeness which is a major segment of the Church's mission in the world.

And that's why a twentieth-century publisher would most likely seize an opportunity to present the reading public with a good book on mentoring even if an eighteenth-century publisher might be tempted to pass it by. He would understand our desperate need to recover the mentoring function and make it the prime activity in all human relationships.

Thank you, Gordon!

Academic Interest in Mentoring on the Rise!

You might also be interested to see the trends of academic interest in the subject of mentoring as documented by Stephen E. Olsen, a Biola University student doing a doctoral dissertation on the subject of mentoring.

> Prior to the 1970s, literature on mentoring was virtually nonexistent. Between 1890 and 1980, Dissertation Abstracts International lists only four dissertations on the subject, whereas between 1980 and 1984, over one hundred dissertations on mentoring are cited in the field of education alone. Gray (1986) notes that over four hundred articles and research studies focused on mentoring in the years between the mid 1970s and 1986. This literature production has continued unabated. In the four years between 1988 and 1992, the Dissertation Abstracts computer database lists 372 dissertations that use mentor as a key word, and between January 1993 and June 1994 alone, there are an additional 153 dissertations on mentoring.

Why Mentoring Is So Important Today

There are at least four major factors that make mentoring so vital for individuals today:
- mobility
- manhood/womanhood
- models
- minority status

Mobility

The mobility of our society makes for a widespread rootless feeling and disconnected relationships. Close family members frequently live five hundred to five thousand miles apart. This leaves most of us hundreds or thousands of miles from aunts and uncles who in times past would naturally have become our mentors. We must make a special effort to develop mentoring relationships.

Manhood/Womanhood

About 30 percent of the male Christian leaders I work with struggle with issues about their manhood. They ask questions such as: "What is a man? How does a boy become a man? When does he know he's a man? Am I a man? How do I know I'm a man?" A mentoring relationship can provide the opportunity for manhood to emerge, to be discussed, to be defined, and to be entered into with a level of confidence that would rarely be possible without the mentoring relationship.

Women, like men, struggle with the process of becoming and feeling like an adult. A mature female mentor can affirm and model adult womanhood at a level one's own mother cannot.

Models

Another reason mentoring is so important today is the acute need for healthy models of adult roles and relationships. You have probably heard the phrases "high tech" and "high touch." The phrases imply that with sophisticated technology comes the increased need for warm relationships to keep life balanced. We have become a hyper-technical society that requires an even deeper touch. We need relationships with a few people at a level we may have never before experienced.

Alvin Toffler, in his book *Future Shock,* put his finger on the fact that when change occurs at such a rapid rate all meaning begins to blur. With the high-tech rate of change, it is even more important that we have a few deep truths and a few deep mentoring relationships that provide some consistency regardless of how much technology, values, social mores, or our own life situations change around us.

We need healthy models of the roles and relationships that adults perform and experience. In our hyper-technical world, the models we often have are people who relate primarily to machinery, megs, RAM, and baud rates. We need models of people who can relate not only to machinery and technology but also to people and to life.

Minority Status

The smaller the group, the more critical it is to nurture, mentor, and keep each leader the group has. If a company has fifty thousand employees, it can lose a few of its leaders and never miss a beat. But a firm of four, forty, or four hundred can't afford to lose a single leader without feeling it deeply. In our generation, Christian leaders are rapidly becoming a minority voice in terms of absolutes, values, perspective, and worldview. We cannot afford to lose a single leader in the Christian community. Thus mentoring has become an even more urgent need in our time.

Why Mentoring Will Be So Important for Our Children and Our Grandchildren

Not long ago, I had the occasion to sit back for a few minutes and reflect on the world into which our children and grandchildren are being born and the environment in which they must grow to maturity. The vision of the world that emerged in my mind was anything but encouraging or pleasant.

I made a list of pressures, temptations, and threats that our children and grandchildren will face. It was a long list. I'm sure you could create a similar one. Most of the items on my list were things my generation did not even think about until we were in our twenties. Most of our children and grandchildren will see them portrayed, modeled, and even encouraged in real life (or in living color on television and movie screens) before they reach high school. Many children will have some degree of exposure to these pressures prior to their first day of kindergarten.

I think you would agree with my conclusion that the world in which our children and grandchildren must grow up is far more difficult than the world we experienced in our own childhoods. For these children to emerge as strong Christian leaders twenty-five years from now, they will have to be prepared, in a sense, as modern "Christian warriors." They won't do battle with guns or bombs but they will have to courageously defend their faith against a wide variety of subtle, blatant, and militant threats.

As I imagined the world of our children and grandchildren, I longed for mentors to come alongside every one of them to help protect them from these threats. Imagine, for a minute, our children and grandchildren growing up in the world they are about to inherit without anyone relating to them, being committed to them, or protecting them. Will they be able to defend themselves alone as they are going through junior high, high school, college, and young adulthood? I don't think so, and they should not have to.

When this reality became clear in my mind, I experienced deep sadness of heart and more than a few tears. For me, mentoring became an even higher priority and deeper passion in my life.

Why Mentoring Will Be Important at the End of Your Life

Jay Kesler, former president of Taylor University, asks, "Who will attend your funeral and not look at their watch?" I think a similar middle-of-the-night question haunts many American adults today: "Will anyone care that I have died, come to my funeral, or even miss me when I'm gone?" Your family, your friends, your mentors, and your protégés will.

This morning I thought of something that I had never considered before. It is not a mathematical formula, it's just an idea that struck me. The total number of tears a person sheds at your funeral may be approximately the same as the total number of tears you two have shared together in life. If you've never cried tears of joy or of sorrow together, I doubt that person will weep at your funeral. But if you have lived the highs and lows of life together, shedding many tears along the way, there will probably be many tears at your funeral. That's the kind of funeral we all want; that's the kind of life we all want to live—a life of significance.

Bottom Line

- Why has mentoring been so significant historically?
- Why is mentoring even more important today?
- Why will it be so important in the future?
- Mentoring is the relational glue that can bond our generation to the previous and the next.
- Mentoring is the bridge that will connect, strengthen, and stabilize future generations of Christians in an increasingly complex and threatening world.

PART TWO

The ABC's of Mentoring

Mentoring does not mean the same thing to everyone. Today, mentoring is a buzz word. It has come to mean everything from a primary professor for a Ph.D. candidate attending Oxford University to a person who helps preschoolers. As a result, many people have only a shallow understanding of what mentoring is really all about. As people give the word more and more meanings, it becomes less and less clearly understood.

In this book I want to encourage a purity of terms. One day soon I hope the word will be clearly understood and properly applied in general conversation and in the definition of programs. When you see or hear a misuse of the term, suggest a synonym: coach, discipler, spiritual guide. Let's make sure *mentoring* means one very special thing.

CHAPTER 3

Mentoring Is...

Realizing that few definitions of any word are absolutely pure, neat, and precise, I want to suggest a definition that explains 99.99 percent of all the mentoring relationships in history, at present, and in the future.

Ideally: *Mentoring is a lifelong relationship in which a mentor helps a protégé reach his or her God-given potential.*

Mentoring is like having an ideal aunt or uncle you respect deeply, who loves you at a family level, cares for you at a close friend level, supports you at a sacrificial level, and offers wisdom at a modern Solomon level. Having a mentor is not like having another mother or father. Mentoring is more "how can I help you?" than "what should I teach you?"

Ideally Mentoring is a Lifelong Relationship

I was once in Boise speaking on mentoring to about four thousand men at Promise Keepers. Two men approached where I was signing books, and one of them said, "Bobb, I just have to tell you! This (pointing to his friend) has been my mentor for thirty years. Now we're friends, but we've been together for thirty years. I knew every day of the last thirty years that this guy cared whether I lived or died." I got tears in my eyes as I listened to them describe what a relationship like that had meant to both of them. What a beautiful relationship!

A TRIBUTE TO MY MENTOR
*By Ed Trenner, Senior Pastor and Senior Consulting
Associate, Masterplanning Group International*

Nothing humbles a man or encourages him like the attention of the one he holds in highest regard.

My mentor is a genius. No one known to me can match his ability to discern, synthesize, create solutions, and give future focus to business or personal concerns. He is a master of perceptive questions. The list of leaders around the world who call on him for insight and advice make an impressive "Who's Who."

Though highly respected, and sought by many, he chose me. He believed in me. Valued my contribution before it had worth to others. Modeled what it means to be a strong servant. Allowed me to ride along to meet the great leaders of our time. He encouraged me, and still does. Provides every resource he has, entrusting the essence of his knowledge and skills. Always asks for my agenda first when meeting. Available day or night, anywhere in the world. Committed to my success. Holds me with an open hand. Seeks my best, helps me be my best, challenges me to more.

We are friends, committed to growing old together.

Ideally, mentoring relationships are forever friendships, but realistically, not all of them last a lifetime. Some very productive mentoring relationships are short-term.

Bruce Johnson, a long-term friend, makes this point: "Hank Williams (the evangelist, not the country singer) asked me to be his mentor. It was the first time anyone had 'officially' asked me. The unknown made it seem like such a big commitment. However, I wanted to help. We agreed to establish a mentoring relationship for one year and outlined the specific areas in which Hank wanted help. Hank's agenda became my agenda.

It has been a year and half since Hank and I ended our 'official' mentoring commitment. Since then Hank calls periodically to ask my advice or to see if I know of anyone who can help him with an issue.

Being a mentor was a positive and comfortable experience. The primary preparation time has turned out to be my own life experiences and a willingness to listen. I am now a mentor to someone else for eighteen months. After that I want to be available to mentor someone else, and then another, and another, for a lifetime of being a mentor.

Bruce Johnson has decided to have an intense mentoring relationship for eighteen months and then to simply remain available for a lifetime. There is nothing wrong with this. In fact, it is a typical pattern for relationships between mentors and protégés. Protégés may have a period of time in which they are in great need. Once helped, they can be on their own for a period of years until they have a great need again, and the mentor is back in the picture. If this is your preferred style, it is a perfectly appropriate form of mentoring. Such a relationship can still be for a lifetime.

People frequently ask me if a lifelong relationship isn't too long anyway, too much to ask, unrealistic. My response is that from the mentor's perspective it may seem that way. But for what the protégé really needs and wants, it is exactly the right amount of time!

Mentoring is a Relationship with Someone You Like, Enjoy, Believe in, and Want to See Win in Life

At its essence, mentoring is a relationship. It is not primarily a contract, a deal, an agreement, or a legal battle if something goes astray. It is a relationship between two people. This is a relationship in which a lot of the public and even the private masks we wear are dropped so mentor and protégé can communicate at a behind-the-mask level.

Ideally, in a mentoring relationship there is a bonding of hearts. There is a commitment of care, support, encouragement, and security. As Bill McCartney, founder of Promise Keepers, puts it, it is moving through life "eye to eye, back to back, and shoulder to shoulder!" The mentoring relationship has many similarities to a marital relationship. Ideally, it is for better or for worse, for richer or for poorer, in sickness and in health. Therefore, it is wise to enter into a mentoring relationship only with someone you like, enjoy being with, believe in, and want to see win in life. I'll say more about this aspect in chapter 16.

Every person is different. Every friendship is different. Every mentoring relationship is different. It involves two people with different backgrounds, different styles, different fears, different interests, and different ages. When you have had one mentoring relationship, don't expect the next to be just like it. You will learn different things from the strengths of each mentor, and you will find yourself teaching different things based on the individual needs of your protégés.

Though when the mentoring relationship begins the mentor is considerably more experienced than the protégé, with time the friendship should grow to be a more balanced, progressively equal friendship. This is what I call the "mutual mentoring" phase. The relationship matures over time into a fifty-fifty emotional partnership. Ideally, the mentor and protégé become friends, mates, pals, and buddies over a period of several years.

A TRIBUTE TO MY MENTOR
Lloyd Murray, Captain
TransWorld Airlines (TWA)

If I could, I would repay what I have taken from my mentor. But, I can't. These are things that can never be repaid . . . just passed on.

Instead, I would say . . .

Thanks for always being willing to listen . . .

Thanks for never making me feel like there was no time for me . . . even though I knew there wasn't . . .

Thanks for being willing to listen to that problem, story, or joke . . .

Thanks for the perspective, which was added at each turn . . .
Thanks for sharing a sandwich . . .
Thanks for sharing what you knew . . .
Thanks for questions . . .
Thanks, mostly, for "just being a friend!"

Mentoring Intentionalizes a Relationship

Most mentoring is informal. It is simply two people who enjoy each other and want to see each other win, helping each other over a period of time. Their relationship involves companionship, camaraderie, correction, and simple friendship. This is natural and appropriate.

So, you may ask, if most mentoring happens on an informal basis, why formalize it? Why try to define the relationship by using the term *mentoring*? Let me give one practical example.

In the process of maturing, there are points at which we need help at inconvenient times. For instance, we might desperately need to talk at 2:00 AM. However, in most relationships, particularly with people we look up to, we would feel uncomfortable calling at two o'clock in the morning. But if you define your mentoring relationship and talk about maturity and health being the bottom-line focus over a lifetime, you can tell your protégé that you are the one person she or he can call at two in the morning. You can tell your protégé to call before doing something foolish like jumping out a window or leaving a spouse. You can make it clear that in an emergency situation, calling you at any hour is not an inconvenience, but a command.

Think about this simple question: Would you feel comfortable calling the two or three people that you want to be your mentors in the middle of the night without permission to do so? Your protégés will not feel comfortable calling you either, even if they are desperate, unless you formalize the fact that your relationship is one of mentoring and assure them that they are free to call.

A Mentor Helps a Protégé Reach Her or His God-Given Potential

Once defined, mentoring is as simple as a natural relationship plus two simple questions. The mentoring relationship becomes significant the moment a person with experience asks a less experienced person what I call the mentoring questions:

- *What are your priorities?* Priorities can be goals or problems. They can be personal or professional.
- *How can I help?* As a mentor, you may need to help your protégé decide on a course of action or simply provide resources to carry it out.

Maturity over a lifetime is the focus. Your mentor, you, and your protégé will always be making progress. Realize that it is a lifelong process, not simply a goal to be reached. God's timing is perfect. Wait for it!

Though it may be frustrating to watch protégés struggle, you may rest easy realizing that you are helping them grow into maturity over a lifetime, not growing them to the point of perfection by the end of the week.

As a part of this maturation over time, you will want to help your protégés achieve steady growth and a basic balance in the following seven areas of life:

- family and marriage
- financial
- personal growth
- physical
- professional
- social
- spiritual

Part of your role as a mentor is helping your protégés reach their potential in life, recognizing, speaking to, and helping correct any serious imbalance in any one of the seven areas.

There have not been enough checklists created to cover every possibility that you or your protégé will face in the next twenty to thirty years. I certainly can't cover all these possibilities in this book. However, if mentors and protégés work together in thinking through issues, praying through problems, and working through difficulties, over time there will be progress toward full, adult, Christian maturity.

Focusing on maturity in mentoring is helpful and healthy. The bottom line is simply this: all you have to do is help your protégés grow into full adult maturity over a lifetime. You may want to ask your protégés, "If you could accomplish only three measurable priorities in the next ten years that would make a fifty percent difference by the end of your life, what would they be?"[1] Then be available to help them reach their priorities. You will have gone a long way toward being a great mentor.

Bill Delahoyde, former Assistant United States Attorney, recounts a moving story of his relationship with his mentor. It's a fitting conclusion to this chapter.

"Could we get together for breakfast tomorrow?" When my mentor asked me that question in 1991, he was speaking to someone who needed a mentor. It had been roughly twenty years since my college campus conversion, and during the interim I had occupied myself as a campus missionary, a seminary graduate, a law school graduate, a 'big firm' associate, and, for almost a decade, a federal prosecutor. But the memorized verses, the seminary education, the seven years of teaching Sunday school, and the passel of books seemed to have left unaddressed a frustrated cynicism that still infected many of my actions and relationships.

During our breakfast together the next morning, he took me through a summary chart from his then soon-to-be-published book. One of the exercises suggested that many of the issues I wrestled with stemmed from deep-seated patterns in my life. I was not going to make progress on those issues until I addressed those patterns. I needed help in this process, and he offered to lend a helping hand. Later I learned that he was really offering to become my mentor."

Mentors are those who have gone before us on the mountain of life, but who pause and extend a hand to help us along the way, or who extend a safety line of love and affirmation that may keep us from falling off the mountain. The mentoring relationship is formed when the mentor turns to the protégé and says, "I love you, I believe in you, I want to help you succeed. I want to make my experience and resources available to help you in any way I can to become all that God wants you to be."

After he became my mentor, we saw each other intermittently over the next two and a half years. On each occasion I'd bring him up to date, and he'd make some suggestions, which I'd try to implement. The next time we got together I'd fill him in on new developments and my progress, or lack thereof.

Through my mentoring relationship with him I came to appreciate the nurturing aspect of mentoring. The definition of nurture is "to promote the development of by providing nourishment, support, encouragement, etc., during the stages of growth." I believe that nurture captures the essence of mentoring because it implies what I would call "warm help." He has helped me in some very tangible ways, but perhaps most importantly, that help was provided in a context infused with loving affirmation. I had tried to get help from various sources over the years, but quite often it was like trying to wring a drop of water out of a damp washcloth: only a slight benefit gained from excessive exertion. I will forever be grateful for his mentoring friendship, which helped initiate a process of replanting my heart in good soil.

One of the last times we were together he commended to me a list of twenty-five character qualities that I would benefit from addressing. But one of the things he said to me on that occasion was, "Bill, this is a ten-year plan. It often takes at least that long to accomplish real change in our lives.

I am finding he was right. But how many of us, unless we are married, have relationships that last ten years? I have benefited greatly from numerous twelve-week plans and nine-month programs, but these experiences always seemed to be missing a crucial ingredient—a relationship that would help me gather together what I had learned and carry it into the future. Since he gave me that list of suggestions, he has moved and I have moved. Moving disrupts our lives, as well as our relationships. But when the dust settles we will get together again and pick up where we left off. Mentoring is like that. It's a relationship that does not end just because you reached the end of a page or an agenda.

Bottom Line

- Mentoring is
    a lifelong relationship,
        in which a mentor
            helps a protégé reach her/his God-given potential.

[1]This is an adaptation of the world-class question Steve Douglass, president of Campus Crusade for Christ, asks: "If we could accomplish only three things in the next ninety days that would make a fifty percent difference, what would we do?"

CHAPTER 4

Mentoring Is Not...

Some aspects of mentoring are similar to certain aspects of other kinds of relationships. Perhaps you're wondering, "What's the difference between mentoring and _____?" Because I think the mentoring relationship is important, unique, and powerful, I want to further clarify the term by speaking to what mentoring is not. When a word is used as loosely in as many sectors as the word mentoring is used, it is sometimes helpful to add clarity to what mentoring is by speaking to what mentoring is not.

- Mentoring is not evangelism or discipleship.
- Mentoring is not an apprentice, big brother, or coaching relationship.
- Mentoring is not modeling.
- Mentoring is not based on matching.

Mentoring Is Not Evangelism or Discipleship

Let me ask you three personal, pointed questions:
- How confident do you feel sharing your faith with a nonbeliever?
- How confident do you feel discipling a new believer?
- How confident would you feel being a lifelong friend to a person you really enjoy?

Perhaps your answer to the first two questions was "very confident."

If so, wonderful! If you evangelize or disciple people regularly, by all means keep evangelizing and discipling. We need every person we can get concentrating on evangelizing and discipling men, women, and children. However, you may have answered the first two questions with something like "not very confident." Thousands of men and women I have met over the past few years believe evangelism and discipleship are critically needed, but when they try to do either they feel they are wearing shoes that don't fit. If you believe in both, but feel like a misfit in either, mentoring may be your ministry niche.

For over twenty-five years I have both had and been a mentor. For over ten years I have been discussing the subject of mentoring with people. The greatest misconception about mentoring is that mentoring is just another word for discipleship. So let me repeat: **mentoring is not discipleship!**

You may find the following chart helpful in seeing the specific differences. Once you see how evangelism, discipleship, and mentoring differ, it will be far easier to identify which is your natural ministry niche.

	EVANGELISM	DISCIPLESHIP	MENTORING
Is it scriptural?	Taught and modeled in Scripture	Taught and modeled in Scripture	Modeled in Scripture
Models in Scripture	Paul	Timothy	Barnabas
How great is the need?	Desperate	Desperate	Desperate
Primary basis of interchange	Content	Content	Relationship
Type of role	Convincing nonbelievers and defending the faith; presenting the Good News	Teaching new believers spiritual truths	Caring for and helping a person in all aspects of life

	EVANGELISM	DISCIPLESHIP	MENTORING
Whose agenda?	Evangelist's agenda (the gospel)	Discipler's agenda (spiritual disciplines)	Protégé's agenda (goals/ problems)
Training required?	Person equipped as evangelist	Academic knowledge and personal mastery of the spiritual disciplines	Practical life experience relevant to protégé
Time frame	Typically, less than one hour	Limited-time course of study	Lifelong as needed
Long-term commitment required	Low	Low	High
Focus of time together	Presenting the salvation opportunity	Teaching the spiritual disciplines	Supporting toward maturity in all areas of life
Importance of personal chemistry	Respect required	Respect required	Respect and personal chemistry both required
Approximate numbers involved	Possibly thousands over a lifetime	Possibly hundreds over a lifetime	Typically one to twelve over a lifetime
Modern role parallels	Brilliant, articulate evangelist/ apologist	Disciplined and mature teacher	Loving aunt, uncle, or more experienced close friend
Essential message	Repent, you must be saved! The kingdom of God is at hand.	To mature spiritually, here is what you need to know, do, or become.	How can I help you get where you are going?

Many people have experienced an ongoing, lifelong relationship with a discipler, and many mentors disciple their protégés. In the chart I am drawing your attention to the significant differences as opposed to the frequent similarities. Categories obviously overlap in the style of some evangelists, disciplers, and mentors. It is helpful to contrast them for clarity. I think you can see how a person might be more suited to one role than another.

Is your natural niche, your giftedness, your comfort zone, your talent, your experience more compatible with:

- evangelism?
- discipleship? or
- mentoring?

I have consulted frequently with the various ministries of Campus Crusade for Christ since 1980. When addressing a group of a few hundred campus staff at a summer training session in Ft. Collins, Colorado, I illustrated the difference between evangelism, discipleship, and mentoring in this way:

> In a year's time, you may see three hundred students come to Christ in your Campus Life program. Out of this three hundred you will probably have thirty that become involved in a leadership program in which you will disciple them over a year's period in the "Ten Steps to Maturity." But when the year is up, you may say, "God bless you. Go in peace!" This is great! You do wonderful work!
>
> Consider what would happen if you chose one to three students out of your discipleship thirty whom you think have the most long-term potential—the greatest heart for God, or the highest potential to lead all of Campus Crusade someday—and say to them, "I'd like to be one of your life mentors." Mentoring can be a logical extension of the discipling process for a few students per year, and the discipling can continue.

This same logic applies to any youth worker (paid or volunteer), teacher, or pastor.

I grew up in the American evangelical subculture. I went to the altar the first time in 1951 when I was eight years old. I remember a time before Billy Graham crusades, Campus Crusade, World Vision, Young Life, Crystal Cathedral, CBN, TBN, Willow Creek Church, Focus on the Family, and Promise Keepers.

If you grew up in a similar time and culture, let me ask, "With how many people from your discipleship program over the last few years do you have a long-term, lifelong relationship today?"

Most people, even staff from organizations that specialize in evangelism and discipleship, say, "I disciple a lot of people through our program. It's my responsibility. I'm faithful to the call. But when the program is over, I lose track of them. I don't have many ongoing relationships."

We desperately need good evangelists, people who share their faith. We desperately need good disciplers, people who will faithfully teach people the spiritual disciplines. But we also desperately need mentors who will commit to a few key people and stand with them for a lifetime, no matter where they go or what they do.

Because we haven't understood the basic distinction between discipleship and mentoring, we have churches full of colleagues in the cause and comrades in the fight, but very few mentors and protégés. We have too few bonded relationships.

When I speak in churches and remark that our pews are filled with "relationally disconnected people," men and women alike instantly start to nod their heads in agreement. That tells me that, on a heart level at least, they understand what's missing. The church is filled with people who work on projects together but don't have the kind of relationship that leads them to shed tears together and to bond at a deep level. What's missing is mentoring.

In their great book, *As Iron Sharpens Iron: Building Character in a Mentoring Relationship,* Howie and Bill Hendricks explain with clarity the role Barnabas played as the apostle Paul's mentor.

The Man Behind Paul

An often overlooked, but crucial hinge on which history turns, is to be found about two hundred miles northwest of Jerusalem on the tiny Mediterranean island of Cyprus. Cyprus was the home of an unassuming Jew named Joses, or Joseph, and it is this man who merits our attention. We don't know how Joses came to faith in Jesus; perhaps he was among the three thousand visitors to Jerusalem at Passover who responded to Peter's proclamation of the gospel (Acts 2). Whatever the circumstances, the message of the Messiah took root in his life, and he began to identify with the early church.

As an indication of his commitment to Christ, Joses sold some or all of his property on Cyprus and brought the proceeds to Jerusalem, where he donated them to the church's benevolence fund. Following custom, the church leaders responded by giving Joses a new (or Christian) name, Son of Encouragement, or Barnabas (Acts 4:36-37).

Now how is it that Barnabas—a relatively minor character in Scripture—could be said to have changed history? The answer is, because Barnabas came to the aid of Saul (later known as Paul) after his dramatic Damascus Road experience and mentored him in the faith. Were it not for Barnabas, who knows what would have happened to Saul—or to the early church? Certainly none of the leaders at Jerusalem wanted anything to do with him. As far as they were concerned, he was "Public Enemy Number One," no matter what happened on the way to Damascus. "But Barnabas," the account reads, "took him and brought him to the apostles" (Acts 9:26-27), defending Saul's claim of conversion, and negotiating access for him to the fellowship of believers.

Barnabas' influence didn't end there. Later, he and Paul traveled together to spread the gospel, and Barnabas apparently promoted Paul to the companions who traveled with them (13:13). Later still, Barnabas challenged Paul over the apostle's treatment of young John Mark (15:36-38). Just because he was known as the Son of Encouragement did not mean that Barnabas avoided conflict.

So while we rightly think of Paul as the strategic spokesman for Christ in the New Testament, we must never forget that behind Paul there was a Barnabas. In fact, Paul seemed to be echoing Barnabas when he wrote to Timothy, "The things you have heard me say in the presence of many witnesses entrust to reliable men who will also be qualified to teach others" (2 Tim. 2:2).

By mentoring Paul, Barnabas was engaging in a ministry of multiplication. The world has never been the same, which demonstrates that every time you build into the life of another person, you launch a process that ideally will never end.[1]

Mentoring Is Not an Apprentice, Big Brother, or Coach Relationship

Just as I believe mentoring is distinct from discipleship, so also I think mentoring is distinct from many other relationships often confusingly referred to as mentoring relationships. The following comparisons may help make the distinctions clear.

MASTER/APPRENTICE	MENTOR
• Primarily focused on work, professional skills	Focused on all of life
BIG BROTHER	**MENTOR**
• Typically, highly social • Occasionally evolves into a relationship that lasts over time • Commitment typically only for six months to a year • A contract more than a genuine long-term relationship	Lifelong relationship
COACH, TEACHER	**MENTOR**
• Typically focused on skill development	Focused on "all of life" development

---

[1]Hendricks, Howard and William, *As Iron Sharpens Iron: Building Character in a Mentoring Relationship* (Chicago: Moody Press, 1995), 129-131.

Friend, Peer, Buddy	Mentor
• Approximately equal experience • Mutual respect • Status quo learning dynamic	• Mentor with much more experience in some area • Protégé admiration for the mentor • Very dynamic learning environment
Hero	**Mentor**
• Hero on a pedestal • No relationship needed • No educational dynamic implied • No caring necessary on the part of the hero	• Mentor admired • Major relational connection • Dynamic learning environment • Mentor cares deeply for the protégé
Spiritual Guide, Advisor, Director	**Mentor**
• Mature spiritual advisor moving beyond the basics • Focused on spiritual areas • Mature long-term relationship approaching that of a mentoring relationship	• Mature advisor focused on all areas of life, including spiritual

Mentoring Is Not Modeling

Modeling is a major part of mentoring, but modeling isn't mentoring. The primary difference between modeling and mentoring is that mentors are personally aware of their protégés and want to use resources to help the protégés reach their God-given potential. However, a person you have never met can be a model for you. A model can work with you closely but see you only as a helper and not one to be helped as a mentor would. A biblical character that you admire can be a model. A famous historical figure can be a model. An author you have never met but from whom you have learned a great deal can be a model. But by definition, none of these people is your mentor.

Modeling is a part of the mentoring process; mentors model life values by the way they live. Mike Downey, founder of Global Missions Fellowship in Dallas, Texas, makes this point very clearly as he talks about his mentor, Dr. C. Sumner Wenip. "Mentors serve as models. Many protégés are plenty motivated—they just need someone who has been around the block a time or two ahead of them to serve as a model.

"Dr. C. Sumner Wenip has been a model of maturity for many years in my own life. As I reflected on how he has influenced my personal development, I looked up 'model' in the dictionary.

"A model is 'a person who represents a standard of excellence to be imitated.' That's exactly how Sumner has mentored me. He represents a standard for me to live up to, and as a result, has had a dramatic impact on my life."

The best father model or mother model many protégés will ever see is their mentor. In many cases, you may be the best model of adulthood your protégé has ever seen.

According to Vickie Kraft, "Many young women today come to Christ who have not been reared in godly homes. They may have had parents who were nominally Christian or attended church, but who at the same time did not demonstrate the life of Christ in their daily routines. These young women don't know what a godly woman, wife, or mother is like, and they need to have that modeled before them. And no one can model a godly Christian woman, except who? A godly Christian woman!"[2]

If all of your adult models have been emotionally imbalanced and spiritually immature, it is hard not to take on that imbalance and immaturity. Modeling within the mentoring relationship can make a major difference! Models aren't necessarily aware that you are watching their behavior, but in a mentoring relationship, the modeling is typically intentional.

Rory Starks, senior vice president of Masterworks, recounts this story which Marty Lonsdale may have forgotten the day after it happened. "Very early in my career I worked for Marty Lonsdale at World Vision. In many ways, Marty was a model even when he wasn't trying to be. I remember being in what I thought was an important meeting with

Marty and other executives. At a specific point in the meeting, Marty said, 'I have a commitment to my son and I have to leave now. Please continue without me.' I was surprised that Marty would leave such an 'important' meeting for his family.

"Today, I have three children of my own. And I've never forgotten Marty's model. Just last week I was in a meeting with my colleagues from around the world in an important meeting. At 4:30 in the afternoon, I said to my colleagues: 'I apologize but I have to leave early. I coach my son's basketball team and I need to honor my commitment to my son to be there this afternoon.'"

A TRIBUTE TO MY MENTOR, STEVE DOUGLASS
by Dr. Allan Beeber, Rev., Ph.D.
Director, WorldLINC Ministries
Global Media Outreach
Campus Crusade for Christ

One of the greatest privileges of my life has been the opportunity to spend time with Dr. Steve Douglass, president of Campus Crusade for Christ.

I am inspired by his consistency, diplomatic ability, and pure motives not to seek his own advantages or misuse his considerable positional authority. I am also the beneficiary of his theological knowledge integrated with common sense and rock solid practicality. What's more, I constantly watch him model a positive, relaxed, Spirit-filled attitude while fulfilling many family obligations and shouldering heavy ministry responsibilities.

Attitudes and values are best learned by modeling within the mentoring relationship. You can learn mathematics, literature, science, and a wide variety of things from a textbook, a computer, or a lecturer. But it is difficult to learn in a classroom setting how to have a new attitude toward a person or a situation. Attitudes are best learned by watching someone you admire and respect model those attitudes.

Modeling plays a major role in teaching attitudes about the value young husbands should put on their wives, the danger of negative kidding plays in a young marriage, the importance of the display of respect and affection of a young wife for her husband, and how to treat a child gently even under pressure. Attitudes, in these situations, will lead to either mature or immature behaviors and reasonable or unreasonable reactions.

I learned many valuable lessons from Dr. Bill Bright, founder and former president of Campus Crusade for Christ. I had the privilege of frequently working with him on a consulting basis beginning around 1980. If I could capture his attitude in a phrase, I'd say Dr. Bright was "more of a cheerleader than a critic." He was one of the most genuinely positive people I have known. He never repeated gossip, never talked critically of a person, and never criticized, but was always looking for the positive.

I learned more by watching Dr. Bright be positive than I have learned by reading books on positive thinking or listening to lectures on positive attitudes. Dr. Bright never turned to me and said, "You know, Bobb, your thinking is negative. You are critical of people. What you just said was gossip according to the scriptural definition." He didn't have to. Simply by watching him, I learned a great deal.

Mentoring Is Not Based on Matching

The mentoring relationship requires a "positive natural chemistry." This cannot be guaranteed and is rarely achieved in the typical computer matching process or by choosing a person out of a crowd. For the short term, one to twelve months, the matching process may work just fine. But for a relationship that lasts a lifetime, the matching process is usually unsuccessful. Shorter-term relationships are more like tutoring big brother/big sister relationships than mentoring relationships. Most attempts at matching can produce deep frustration when the relationships must last more than one semester or some other brief, specific commitment period.

A protégé is someone you like, enjoy, believe in, and want to see win in life. He or she is someone for whom you're willing to sacrifice and whom you would love to have as a son or daughter, cousin, niece or nephew, or grandchild.

A quick note: some people, like the old matchmaker in *Fiddler on the Roof,* have a good eye for people who are especially compatible and can introduce people who seem to have a good chance of developing the positive natural chemistry required. But this is a *rare* gift.

Five Common Misconceptions about Mentoring

Misconception number one: *Mentors are at least eighty-three years old.*

One of the most common misconceptions about mentoring involves age. Many people assume that in order to be old enough, wise enough, and mature enough to be a mentor, you have to be at least eighty-three years old. They assume the only appropriate protégés are sixteen-year-olds receiving their tutelage on a stuffed leather bench at a grand piano. This is simply not the case.

A mature sixteen-year-old can easily understand the concept of mentoring and take on one or two younger students as protégés. This happens often but is not usually referred to as mentoring. Challenge a young leader you know to become a mentor.

On the other hand, age eighty is not too old to be a mentor. In fact, age one hundred and ten is fine if you have a sound mind and a caring heart! Bo Mitchell is one of my closest friends. We have gone through many good and bad times together over the past fifteen years or so. When I asked Bo if he would care to do a tribute, he smiled and said, "My tribute would be to Doc Taylor!"

Doc Taylor was eighty-nine years old when we first met. He was one of my best friends for ten years until he died forty days short of his one hundredth birthday. He taught me about marriage, about business, about being a father, and about being a friend.

I called him an average of three to four times a week for ten years to check and see if he was okay. When I called Doc, his first response to my "Doc, this is Bo" was always the same: "Bo, just this minute I was praying for you!" One day I asked him, "How can it be possible that every single time I call you have just been praying for me?" As long as I live I'll never forget his answer: "Bo, you are always in my thoughts, and the best thing I can do for you is lift your name to God all day long." When he passed away I lost a ton of prayer support and a great life mentor.

In Doc Taylor, God gave me a prayer partner, friend, and mentor who was constantly thinking about me and what was best for me. I have now lost him on earth. But what he taught me I will never forget. . . . As I remember Doc's life and wisdom, things he said keep coming back to my memory, and I am confident his life will continue to teach and mentor me as long as I live.

I'd advise you to ignore age when selecting a mentor. Just look for a person who has more experience (personal or professional) than you, a person whom you respect and like a lot, and from whom you want to learn.

Younger protégés look at mentors as "older," but mentors look at protégés over thirty simply as "adult." As a protégé, you may be constantly aware of the age difference. If you are over thirty, your mentor probably sees you as a young adult friend. The relationship is adult to adult, not adult to child.

Misconception number two: *Mentors must be perfect!*

This misconception causes qualified people to hesitate about becoming mentors. The fact is, protégés don't expect a mentor to be perfect.

I once spoke at a conference where I asked how many of the attendees expected their mentors to be perfect. Not one hand went up. Then I asked, "How many of you have procrastinated about becoming a mentor because you assumed that you had to be perfect as a mentor?"

Probably 95 percent of the hands in the room went up. The bottom line is mentors are not perfect, and they don't need to be.

At the Third Annual National Mentoring Conference (1994) sponsored by Mentoring Today in Portland, Oregon, protégés used the following words and phrases to describe their mentors:

- consistent, stable
- affirming
- believed in me
- accepted me where I was
- saw me as a person of value
- included me in his life
- fun
- a person of character, trustworthy
- I admired the mentor
- there was a naturally positive relationship between us
- I knew my mentor was not perfect—didn't matter

No one who participated in the discussion expected their mentors to be anywhere near perfect. All the protégés cared about was, "Does this person care for me and want to see me win in life?"

While you may be a perfectionist, mentoring is one thing that you *do not* have to do perfectly. In fact, there isn't any way to do it perfectly. You don't have to be 100 percent competent or 100 percent correct. All you have to do is care and, as much as possible, be there when your protégé needs help.

Misconception number three: *Mentors have all the answers.*

This misconception is obviously related to the one before it. The same logic applies. Mentors are human. They do not have all the answers. They will never have all the answers. Their role is sometimes to be the answer, sometimes to have the answer, but most of the time to know where to find the answer.

Fundamentally, a mentor connects a protégé to resources: his or her personal network, appropriate seminars, libraries, helpful audio or visual materials, and even support groups. The mentor is never required to have all the answers or all the resources. He or she is simply a connector to many resources that the protégé needs during the growth process.

As a mentor, your attitude should be, "I'm here to help you, and I'll do what I can."

The appendices of this book will help you to help your protégé find the answers. They suggest additional resources that you may turn to when a protégé asks you, "Where can I find help in decision making, problem solving, risk taking, hiring, firing, or focusing my future?"

Misconception number four: *The mentoring process involves a curriculum the mentor teaches a protégé.*

Believe me, no such curriculum exists. The mentoring process is unique to each protégé. Learning is based on the protégé's agenda, priorities, questions, and needs—not on the mentor's preset program.

Within a trust relationship, protégés are able to ask questions they would never feel comfortable asking most people. They learn best when their need to know is greatest. Therefore, the single most teachable moment of any protégé's life is the few seconds immediately following a sincere question. No curriculum, checklist, or theory could replace a mentor's life experience and compassion in such a teachable moment.

Misconception number five: *A mentor's focus is holding a protégé accountable.*

My observation is that many people focus on accountability for one of two reasons: they enjoy holding other people accountable but do not particularly want to be held accountable themselves, or they lack self-control and try to put that responsibility in someone else's hands. Obviously, both of these motivations are unhealthy and would be detrimental to a mentoring relationship. Accountability should not be the focus of the mentoring relationship. The focus should be supporting, strengthening, and encouraging.

Of course, in the natural process of helping the protégés grow to maturity, you will use an element of accountability. For instance, you can hold your protégé accountable for following through on something if a little accountability support helps to form a new habit, reach a new goal, or resist some temptation. But do not feel that, as a mentor, you are supposed to hold your protégés accountable every step of the way.

Their accountability needs to be developed in terms of responsibility to God, government, and other legitimate authorities, not to you.

Bottom Line

- Mentoring doesn't mean the same thing to everyone.

- Mentoring is not evangelism, discipleship, or modeling.

- Mentoring is commonly misunderstood today.

- Mentoring is a lifelong relationship in which a mentor helps a protégé reach her/his God-given potential.

[1]Kraft, Vickie, *Women Mentoring Women: Ways to Start, Maintain, and Expand a Biblical Women's Ministry* (Chicago: Moody Press, 1992), 27.

CHAPTER 5

Twenty-one of the Most Frequently Asked Questions about Mentoring

Practically speaking, what is keeping you from becoming a mentor or seeking one? As I talk with literally hundreds of individuals each year about mentoring, I find that most postpone mentoring because of mental bogeymen, natural fears, or irrational ideas. These small things keep mature, capable people with much to offer from taking the first mentoring steps. Usually a little practical information helps people get past the bogeymen. I hope you won't let fears or doubts keep you from pursuing a genuinely satisfying relationship with a mentor or a protégé.

If I were one of your mentors, I'd tell you to feel free to ask me anything. Since I can't be with you in person, I want to share the questions I've been asked most often and give you my answers.

1. Who initiates the mentor/protégé relationship?

Ideally, a mentor takes the first step in the mentoring relationship by offering to help the protégé succeed. Ideally, the mentor seeks, chooses, and approaches the protégé because the mentor is committing to a lifetime of attention, interest, and encouragement. That's a major commitment!

Realistically, a protégé may need to approach a mentor. Some potential mentors do not feel confident initiating the relationship. They are hesitant to approach you and say, "I'd like to be your mentor." Often, these are the most capable, compassionate people—the very kind of person you need.

My advice is to be realistic: don't wait for your ideal mentors to come to you. Go to them and say, "You are a person I have respected and looked up to for a long time. I'd like to talk with you about the possibility of you becoming one of my life mentors."

If they ask what you mean by the word mentoring, you may want to hand them a copy of this book. Say something like "Please read this, and next Wednesday, let's have breakfast to explore the possibility of you being one of my mentors." When you've both read the same material, you have a clearer idea of what you're really asking.

A good mentoring relationship may exist naturally but could be made stronger if the mentor or the protégé initiated a discussion about a more formal relationship. Typically, each person is uncertain about how to approach the other to discuss the mentoring relationship. The mentor is silently wondering, *Do I have anything to offer this exceptionally gifted person?* The protégé is silently asking, *Why would this outstanding person want to help me?*

Don't wait. Initiate—as a mentor or a protégé!

2. How Much Time Does a Mentoring Relationship Require?

Every mentoring relationship takes a different amount of time. Some people can meet once a week, some once a month, some once a quarter. I see some of my protégés only once a year, others once every two or three years. I would enjoy seeing them much more frequently, but time and distance do not allow it. Each relationship may vary from year to year in the amount of time it requires.

The amount of time required in your mentoring relationship depends on your situation and your needs. Whatever you can both afford and agree on is fine.

Skip Lewis has a great perspective on the informal side of the mentoring relationship: "Another component that protégés registered in my research was the need for outside contacts with their mentors. Each of the respondents expressed appreciation for seeing mentors outside of the usual meeting times. Nancy mentioned how her friendship with Diane was forged in shopping trips and in doing crafts together, where they 'talked about everything in the world.' This made Diane's [the mentor's] confrontational posture easier to handle for Nancy, because 'I know Diane loves me.' Pete remarked how exciting it was to see his mentors share Christ with a waitress while they ate lunch together. Pete noted 'It was great seeing them in action and dealing in a secular setting. That was really exciting.'" Obviously, when all you can do is "invite your protégé along," even that will be meaningful.

Reality check: Mentoring does take time. Occasionally it will be inconvenient and somewhat out of your comfort zones. But it will be well worth it!

3. What Do We Talk about When We Meet?

At each session, however frequently you agree to meet, the mentor may want to start with the mentoring questions: "What are your priorities?" and "How can I help?" The protégé should come to each meeting prepared to discuss:

- pressing decisions about which the mentor can give perspective
- problems in reaching the priorities with which the mentor can help if possible
- plans for the mentor's general information and update
- progress points for the mentor's update so the mentor can give well-deserved praise
- prayer requests for the mentor's prayers and general support
- personal roadblocks, blind spots, and other concerns

Note one: The problems, decisions, and plans are typically related to the protégé's priorities in the seven areas of life mentioned earlier.

Note two: To simplify your meetings even more, before each meeting the protégé should make an exhaustive list of questions he or she is trying to answer—ideally in priority order. The protégé can ask the mentor for advice or comment on each question. Discussion can follow as time allows and need requires.

Note three: Protégés—the more eager you are to learn and the more you express appreciation when you do, the more willing your mentors will be to teach you the very best they know on any subject!

4. Can I Have More than One Mentor?

God frequently uses not one mentor but several mentors to help a person in the process of growing towards full maturity. I've talked with a number of Christian leaders who tell me this is a very common experience.

The following tributes will give you an idea of how God has used multiple mentors in the maturing process of several Christian leaders.

A TRIBUTE TO THE MEANINGFUL MENTORS IN MY LIFE
by Paul Cedar, President
Mission America

Although I have never had a formal relationship with a mentor, God has been gracious to allow me to have a number of meaningful mentoring relationships with key Christian leaders who have made a significant investment in my life and ministry. It is interesting to note that each of them made different kinds of contributions.

My first mentoring relationship was with Charlie Riggs, the director of counseling and follow-up for the Billy Graham Evangelistic Association. God used Charlie to help me develop a profound commitment to the ministry of God's Word, obedience to the God of that Word, and a deep love for lost people.

During the years I had the privilege of ministering with Leighton Ford, that dear brother contributed to my life in so many ways. He helped me learn to share the Gospel with contemporary people in a clear, articulate way with the love of Christ and the power of the Holy Spirit.

As I ministered with Lloyd Ogilvie for some five years,

God used him in many ways in my life including his focus on excellence—and his commitment to do all to the glory of God.

The deepest mentoring relationship in my life has been with Ted Engstrom. It began in my early days of ministry as a Youth for Christ director and has continued through the ten years that I had the privilege of being Ted's pastor to the present day. God has used Ted to teach me a great deal about how to administrate effectively, to communicate clearly, and to be involved in accountability relationships both formal and informal.

I thank God for these brothers and for the many other faithful Christian men and women who invested in my life and ministry—to the glory of God!

Jim Hiskey, a lifelong friend of mine, has had four outstanding mentors in his life:

Four very dear special friends have had a major effect in mentoring me in Christ. First Bill Bright, who imparted to me two major things: First, vision. Bill often said things like, "Small dreams do not inflame the hearts of men." And second, a piece of wisdom that has always stayed with me for the past thirty-five years: "Things are not always the way they appear to be," he said, "so make sure you have all the facts before you make a judgment."

The second brother, Doug Coe, has had such an impact on me that it would be very difficult to cite one or two areas in which he has impacted me. The first, however, has to be his emphasis on the Great Commandment and the Great Commission. Doug has often asked: "Can there be a greater purpose in life than to love God with all your heart, mind, soul, and strength and to love your neighbor as yourself?" Of course we agreed over thirty years ago there could be none and have given ourselves to that great commandment.

Second, Doug has modeled to me someone who takes seriously Christ's commandment to "disciple all nations." He himself has prayed for every nation of the world and traveled to more than 250 in order to find "a laborer" and then to build a core of disciples around that laborer. One other thing I've learned from Doug is the power of two or three. Doug often quotes the verses "How could one chase a thousand and two put ten thousand to flight" (Deut. 32:30, NKJV) and "a threefold cord is not quickly broken" (Eccles. 4:12, NKJV). Two or three banded together in Christ can effect powerful consequences as seen in Peter, Silas, and Luke or in Shadrach, Meshach, and Abednego. Doug has been a tremendous model on these and has helped me to see this.

The third brother, Dick Halverson, taught me also the power of two or three, but his emphasis was slightly different. Regarding prayer Jesus says, "If two of you agree on earth concerning anything that they ask, it will be done for them by My Father in heaven" (Matt. 18:19, NKJV). Again I've learned the power of two or three having genuine spiritual agreement. There are many things I have learned from Dick. He is such a great example of a person with a strong devotional life. I've often heard him say that he'd be out of business if he didn't have that hour a day with the Lord. I've quizzed him about this often and have observed him doing things I've never seen anyone else do. For one thing, he has photographs of people he prays for every day. Dick also said that "all progress in Christ is measured downward." He has been reading Oswald Chambers every day for over fifty years. This is one of Chamber's key principles in life.

The last brother, Jim Houston, has helped me as much as anybody to see the importance of head and heart being married together. As the Psalmist says, mercy and truth are met together. Jim spoke often to us, as we had the pleasure to form the C. S. Lewis Institute here in Washington, about the integration of our faith with vocation, which he calls another marriage. More than that, Jim models head and heart, faith, and vocation centered in Jesus.

Obviously, multiple mentors are both common and desirable.

5. Where is the Best Place to Meet?

Most mentoring takes place in a relaxed setting: walking, sailing, golfing, driving—anywhere you are with your mentor or your protégé. Mentoring often happens ten minutes at a time, here and there as you move through life together. Don't see mentoring as all work. It often involves the joy of mutual sharing. Mentoring happens more in the context of a relationship than in a formal classroom. As much a life attitude as a formal structure, it can be even more enjoyable as you do things together!

Ross Goebel served as my executive assistant for a year. Though there is a thirty-year difference in our ages, we enjoy some of the same pastimes. Some of our very best conversations have happened on the rocks in the Dana Point Harbor just watching the sailboats go by and discussing life. Another great time was when he and I spontaneously decided to drive from Orlando the forty-five miles over to the platinum coast of Florida to watch a space shuttle launch at the Kennedy Space Center. We discussed twenty-five topics if we discussed one, just chatting along on our way to a launch and back.

Avoid artificial or formal settings and meet wherever you are most comfortable.

6. If I'm Mentoring Preteens, Should I Tell Them I'm Their Mentor?

Generally speaking, no. Simply be a friend. Be available. Ask about their thoughts for the future and how can you help, but don't formalize the relationship. You can easily say, "If you ever need anything, give me a call." One Sunday school teacher in Brooklyn Park, Minnesota, gave each of her fourth graders a quarter and said, "You keep this, and don't spend it, but here's my phone number. If you ever need any help in your life, give me a call." You can do those kind of things, but I would suggest, as a rule of thumb, don't use the term *mentor* with someone under sixteen years.

7. How Can a Mentor and a Protégé Avoid Becoming Competitive?

Wise protégés choose to use their newfound understanding to excel in areas that are different from their mentors' areas of expertise, strength, or market. If you are a young doctor honing your skills and you open a medical practice just down the street from your M.D. mentor, he or she will see it as competition, regardless of how loving she is toward you. If you are going to make a living from the information your mentor shares with you, ask your mentor if he or she feels you would be competing. Make sure you make your living in a way that does not threaten your mentor's income.

8. When Do I Get to Teach My Values to My Protégés?

In the process of helping your protégés reach their goals, frequently they will ask, "Is there anything else I should know or be aware of right now?" At these teachable, mentoring moments, gently share any other helpful perspective or wisdom you care to convey.

Always start by mentioning some things they are doing right. Then, point out areas where the protégé needs to grow personally. For example, you might gently address irritating habits, poor attitudes, spiritual insights, appearance, or even personal hygiene. Just remember to stay focused on your protégés' agendas.

9. Should I Ever Tell My Protégés What They Should Do?

If you keep asking, "What are your priorities?" and "How can I help?" I guarantee there will come a day when your protégé will turn to you and ask, "Well, what do you think?" At that point you are free to make comments or suggestions. But be careful not to use that as a once-and-for-all license to tell your protégé what you think. Share your ideas on the topic at hand, and then wait to be asked again.

Occasionally, protégés make plans or decisions that are obviously self-destructive or unwise. You should feel 100 percent free to express your concerns and bring your perspective to bear in such situations. You are not telling them what to do. You are simply giving them the benefit of your experience.

Steve Woodworth, the brilliant president of Masterworks in Poulsbowa, Washington, had just such an encounter.

> Several mentors have helped me immensely, but one encounter stands out above all others. I had just become a partner in a young, growing company. I met with my mentor to talk through how to grow the company and ensure success.
>
> After several hours of talking about my business, he shifted the focus. My wife and I had just adopted twin infants, and he said something I will never forget. "Bond with your babies while they are young." He warned me not to fall into the trap he'd seen so many men fall into working hard to build a financial foundation, thinking that they would spend time with the kids when they were older. He'd seen many men end up never bonding with their children.
>
> I decided to spend at least an hour a day focused on the children, even before they could walk or talk. Within a month, I had a far more intense love for the twins. I've kept that commitment almost every day since. I'm now reaping the rewards of a deep emotional bond with Joel and Heather.

10. How Do I Deal with My Fear of Being Rejected in a Mentoring Relationship?

Different people have different levels of fear of rejection. In the book *Why You Do What You Do*, I explain that everyone has fears, but not everyone has the same kind of fear. Some people have very little fear of rejection, but for other people it's a constant dread. If your concern is of personal rejection, you may find it easier not to mention the word *mentoring* for the first year or two. Simply try to play the role of a mentor in a person's life, or just spend extra time with the respected adult if you want to be a protégé.

There's nothing wrong with spending time with a person to move the trust level higher and higher, to the point that you can formalize the mentoring relationship. If you are concerned about rejection, wait to discuss the subject. Just relate, relax, enjoy, build, and grow together, and at the right time, using the word *mentoring* will make sense.

11. How Do I Get Out of a Mentoring Relationship?

Ending a mentoring relationship is no different than ending any other kind of relationship. It is a tough interpersonal issue. There are three key words to use when you are dealing with an interpersonal issue: *care, honesty,* and *fairness.* Use them together something like this: "I *care* far too much about you not to be *honest* with you, and in *fairness* to you we need to slow down, stop, change, or redefine our mentoring relationship." Then explain why.

Sometimes people who ask this question are concerned about confrontation. Most people get uneasy, uptight, insecure, and anxious when they have to confront someone. It helps me to substitute the word *clarify* for *confront.* Instead of confronting anyone ever again, simply clarify issues with them. For example, to redefine or terminate a mentoring relationship that has not met your expectations, you could say, "I *care* far too much about you not to be *honest* with you, and I need to clarify how I felt when you said that; I need to clarify the assumptions I was making; I need to clarify the agenda; I need to clarify the expectations I had for our relationship that led to my disappointment." The word *clarify* is a lot easier to face than the word *confront.*

Stephen E. Olsen adds a very wise perspective: "When a relationship comes to closure (due to a move or some other life circumstance), I have found it very helpful to verbally define it simply as a new phase of our relationship. It doesn't mean an end; it simply means a continuation under different circumstances. This keeps it open for a variety of ways of relating. This is especially helpful when the relationship has been exceptionally intimate."

12. Should a Mentor Ever Lend Money to a Protégé?

Let me strongly urge you never to lend or borrow money in a mentoring relationship. Do not ask your mentor for money. Do not imply that you will give money to a protégé. The minute money comes into a relationship, the relationship can get confusing, awkward, explosive, and embarrassing. The danger in loaning protégés money is similar to the danger in loaning relatives money. It can be disruptive to the relationship and can cause the relationship to deteriorate quickly. I cannot overstate the case: caution, caution, caution!

13. Is it Possible for a Husband to Mentor His Wife, or Vice Versa?

It's possible, but dangerous. I think it is unwise for a husband to call himself his wife's mentor, and I do not recommend it. Besides, discovering her agenda and helping her to accomplish her dreams is the role of a husband as well as a mentor, so there is no need to call him a mentor.

The same could be said of a wife toward her husband. A wife may have a lot of extraordinarily helpful experience to share with her husband. Cheryl and I have discussed how much stronger I am because of having been married to her since 1964. The strength she has brought to me is immeasurable. She has said that I have brought strength to her as well. A healthy, mature couple will build into each other. I would not call it a mentoring relationship, but rather a husband and wife relationship.

14. What Should I Do if My Protégé or My Mentor Fails?

No protégé wants to fail, but sometimes a protégé needs a mentor's help to know how to succeed and how to learn from failure. A wise mentor expects a protégé to be less than perfect, especially in the formative years. A protégé should have no fear of being rejected by the mentor. It is helpful for the mentor and the protégé to discuss failure, including the freedom to fail and not be rejected, in general terms before the inevitable failure occurs.

Likewise, no mentor wants to fail. A wise protégé expects a mentor to be less than perfect. A mentor should have no fear of being rejected by the protégé. It may surprise you as a protégé to hear that your mentor might fear being rejected by you, but it is common. Ask yourself, do you fear being rejected by your protégé? The same concern is typically experienced by your mentor. Be sensitive to your mentor at this point.

15. What Should I Do if the Mentoring Relationship Becomes Destructive?

If, for whatever reason, the mentoring relationship becomes dysfunctional, it is best simply to abandon the relationship as quickly as possible and to find a healthier relationship. This is not always easy, and you may need the help of a pastor or a mutual friend to disentangle yourself from the relationship.

If you feel that your mentor or protégé is beginning to take unfair advantage of you, I suggest the following steps:
- Pray about the situation; ask for God's wisdom.
- Talk it over; get your feelings into the open.
- Talk with a close friend who can keep a confidence; ask your friend for wisdom and perspective on your relationship.

A mentoring relationship should be constructive, not destructive. If you feel that your relationship is becoming destructive, at the very least you need to redefine your relationship.

16. Is Mentoring at a Distance Possible?

Yes, mentoring can take place at a distance. The main questions are: "Do I really believe in this person?" and "Do I want to see her or him succeed?" If the answer to both questions is yes, you can help in many ways, even at a distance via mail, fax, e-mail, telephone, and occasional personal visits.

17. How Confident Do Most People Feel about Becoming Mentors?

Most adults feel somewhat intimidated by the prospect of becoming a mentor, and do not realize how effective they could be when working with inexperienced, eager protégés. At the same time, most adults can quickly name three young people who might benefit from their support and encouragement. The vast majority of adults say they would have benefited from such supportive relationships in their lives while they were younger.

Whatever you do, don't let a little discomfort keep you from approaching one to three young people to offer your mentoring support. They need your experience, wisdom, and encouragement!

18. What Should I Do if My Mentor or Protégé Doesn't Follow through with Our Original Agreement?

Stay positive! Assume the mentor or protégé wants to get together but is just busy. Take the initiative. Don't wait and let your fears and anxiety build. The problem could be just a difference of assumptions or a busy schedule, not personal rejection. Do not read rejection into a silence or a distance. Chances are about 99 percent that you are not being rejected!

You may need to redefine your relationship to require less time or agree to a meeting time that is better for both of your schedules. Don't give up, just redefine.

19. What if the Protégé Outgrows the Mentor?

Frequently, great pain comes into the mentoring relationship, and a broken relationship occurs. Ideally, however, the relationship changes from mentor-protégé to friends (mutual mentors), and the mentor is honored to see the protégé succeed, much as fathers and mothers are honored by the success of their children in adulthood.

20. Can I be a Mentor if I Have Never Had One?

Absolutely. You will find it harder than if you had a mentor as a model, but it is no more impossible than being a good father when you didn't have a healthy, balanced father. If you have experience and encouragement to share and the desire to mentor, by all means do it.

21. Should I Automatically Consider My Staff Members as Protégés?

No! You should have a basic leadership development checklist for each of your staff members to follow. You may want to share your list of the ten best books, tapes, or videos on leadership. You can give them assignments that stretch them and cause them to grow. But unless the basic mentor and protégé chemistry is present, the mentoring relationship will not work.

On the other hand, just because people are on your staff does not automatically disqualify them as protégés either. If you believe in one or more of them and want to see them succeed in life, go ahead! Offer to be a mentor.

CHAPTER 6

Anyone Can Mentor, But Not Everyone Should

You can be a mentor by helping someone who has ability and a teachable attitude but less experience than you. For example:

- A senior citizen can mentor a mature adult.
- A mature adult can mentor a young adult.
- A young adult can mentor a college student.
- A college student can mentor a high school student.
- A high school student can mentor one in junior high.
- Anyone who really wants to can become a mentor!

Anyone Can Mentor

Remember the George Caywood story? (His father committed suicide when George was only fifteen.) Our conversation and George's story continues.

Seeking more clarity about the mentor who could have made a difference, I said, "George, let me ask you this. How smart would that man have had to be?"

By that time he had gotten his composure a little bit, and he said, "Bobb, that guy could have dropped out of the first grade, and I wouldn't have cared a bit."

I said, "How high a position would he have had to have?"

He said, "He could have been a homeless bum. I wouldn't have cared."

I said, "George, how handsome would he have had to be? Would he have had to have been fit and trim and everyone's ideal of what a man is?"

Exasperated, George said, "Bobb, stop asking me these questions. You know the answers. There were no criteria of any kind when I was fifteen. The only criterion I would have used that day was, 'Does this man care for me?' That would have been it!"

I asked, "George, how would you have felt about that man today?"

He said, "He would have been at every one of my award dinners. I've gotten lots of awards, but there's been no mentor sitting there."

Every time I've ever mentioned the word *church* to George, his jaw has tightened just a bit. Now understand, this man speaks in churches a lot, he's been a pastor, and he's a man committed to things of God. He knows more Scripture by heart than most people I have met. He's committed to building God's church.

I said, "George, how would you have looked at the church differently if just one guy had done that?"

He said, "I can't even comprehend how I would have looked at it differently."

I said, "The men of your church didn't know what to say, so they just said nothing, right?"

He said, "Yeah, I understand. As an adult I understand. As a kid I didn't understand. I just got angry with them."

George had no requirements about what a mentor should be when he was fifteen. Neither do fifteen or fifty-year-olds today. You don't have to be handsome, beautiful, educated, rich, or socially skilled to be very meaningful to a kid who has no one or to a kid who looks up to you in some way. Anyone can be a mentor!

There is another great story about mentoring told by a highly respected man. As you read his story, ask yourself, "What did it take to be the mentor of Professor Howard Hendricks when he was a child?"

> I was born into a broken home in the city of Philadelphia. My parents were separated before I was born. I never saw them together except once in my life: when I was called to testify in a divorce court in the city of Philadelphia. And I'm sure I could have been born, reared, died, gone to

hell, and nobody would have particularly cared, except a small group of believers got together in my neighborhood to found an evangelical church, and that was a miracle because everybody said, "You can't found an evangelical church in that community." You know, whenever somebody says, "You can't do it," I often think I hear God roar, "Oh really? Watch me!"

That small group of individuals met to worship, and to study, and to develop a passion for that community. A man by the name of Walt came to the Sunday School superintendent and said, "I want to teach a Sunday School class."

He said, "Wonderful, Walt, but we don't have any boys. You go out into the community, and anybody you pick up, that's your class."

Walt went out. I'll never forget the day I met him. He was six feet, four inches tall. He said to me, as a little kid, "Hey, son, how would you like to go to Sunday School?" Well, anything that had "school" in it had to be a bad news item! And then he said, "How would you like to play marbles?" Oh! That was different! Would you believe we got down and played marbles till he beat me in every single game? I lost my marbles early in life. And by the time he got through, I didn't care where he was going; that's where I wanted to go.

He picked up thirteen of us boys, nine of us from broken homes. Today, all thirteen of us are in full-time vocational Christian work. And Walt never went beyond sixth grade.

I can't tell you a thing he ever said. I can tell you everything about him, because he loved me more than my parents did. He loved me, for Christ's sake. And I'm moving today because of a man who not only led me to Christ, and discipled me, but started that mentoring process.

Your protégé can be a person with extremely high potential or someone who would not "make it in life" without your help!

Not Everyone Should Mentor

If Walt could mentor, theoretically anyone can. However, not everyone has a personality suited to mentoring. Some people are highly egocentric. In their minds, the whole world revolves around them, and it has since they were children. This is diametrically opposite to the mentoring relationship, in which the protégé is the center, so to speak, and the mentor actually revolves around the protégé's agenda. People who are egocentric typically do not make good mentors and should not feel guilty if they do not become mentors.

As we saw earlier, others are humble and secure but are more gifted as evangelists or disciplers than as mentors. These people might be aggressive evangelists or wise disciplers, but they are not relational mentors in the way that we have been discussing. Don't fight who God made you to be. If God made you an evangelist by nature, be an evangelist. If He made you a discipler by nature, be a discipler. But if He made you a mentor by nature, be a mentor.

Consider your phase of life. Some people are in phases of life that make it unwise for them to be mentors. The focus, energy level, and ability to be a balanced mentor varies in three phases in life.

The Survival Phase

If you are just trying to pay the bills or are under so much pressure that you have no reserve left at the end of the day to give to anyone, your focus is on surviving. The survival phase is rarely the time to become a mentor.

You may be in an extremely stressful period of life. Perhaps your business is falling apart, or your family is falling apart, or you're just hanging on by your fingertips. Please, *get* a mentor, but don't worry about *becoming* one.

When I turned forty, I was so discouraged with life that I told my wife, Cheryl, "If you give me a surprise party, I'll just walk out. I don't want to see anyone. I am so discouraged right now. I am so tired. I am so exhausted. I have nothing left to give anyone." At that point, I was just surviving. I was in no shape to mentor anyone. Fortunately, ten years later, she was able to surprise me on my fiftieth birthday and things were wonderful! I know what it feels like to have nothing left to give. And if you're there, you may say, "I believe in this mentoring thing, and Billy down the street really needs me, but I haven't got anything to give." Don't feel guilty. Don't try to begin a mentoring relationship. Just wait. Things will change.

The Success Phase

You may be in a phase where success is your focus, where your company, your church, or your responsibilities are growing so fast that to take on another responsibility would be "schedule suicide." Like the survival phase, the success phase is probably not the best time for you to become a mentor. Until you can shift some priorities, don't jump into mentoring.

The Significance Phase

You may be asking yourself, "How can I make the most difference?" You may be in a mid-life reevaluation phase where you are feeling a great need for deeper relationships. You may have retired early, have achieved financial independence, or for some other reason have time on your hands. You are in the significance phase. Now is the time for you to consider mentoring.

Whatever phase you are in, wait until it's appropriate to start mentoring, but don't wait until it feels totally comfortable; it may never feel totally comfortable to walk up to someone and say, "I care whether you live or die."

In short, wait until you really want to be a mentor and don't feel any pressure from me, or anyone else to become one. Wait for God's perfect timing!

Bottom Line

- Mentoring is something anyone can do.
- Mentoring is something not everyone should do, at least now!
- When it's your time, mentoring is a very significant thing to do.

CHAPTER 7

Warnings

Have you ever heard of a mentoring relationship that did not work out as well as the mentor and protégé had originally hoped? Some mentoring relationships do "blow apart" just as some marriages do, no matter how great the honeymoon! Occasionally what two eager people had hoped would be a lifelong relationship disintegrates, drifts apart, or just dies for lack of natural chemistry. There are three common reasons for such disappointing results. I call them the Big Three Mentoring Misfires:

- mentoring the opposite sex
- having a non-Christian mentor
- starting with unrealistic expectations

The good news is all three can be avoided!

Mentoring the Opposite Sex

I met Bill Bright in 1963, and I've consulted with the Campus Crusade for Christ team on a fairly regular basis since 1980. I asked Bill only two personal favors in all the time I worked with him. (He offered to do many more. Bill was a very generous servant.) One favor resulted in an important piece of advice.

One day I handed him a copy of the manuscript for the booklet *Mentoring: How to Find a Mentor and How to Become One* and said,

"Bill, I need you to read this because I really need your wisdom on it. I need your counsel. I want to introduce it to the Crusade movement, and I don't want to introduce anything that's diametrically opposite to your thinking."

When he read it, he was very positive. Bill was a very positive, encouraging person. However, he suggested one addition. He said, "I would advise against a man ever mentoring a woman."

Like other helping relationships, mentoring relationships get deep enough, fast enough that the love individuals give and receive can easily be reinterpreted into sexual dimensions. We can find ourselves attracted to a mentor or protégé of the opposite sex—even if the person isn't that physically attractive to us. The relationship can present more intimacy than we have with other people, and it can get emotionally and sexually confusing. I agree with Bill: I definitely recommend against mentoring the opposite sex!

Realistically speaking, the imbalance between women who want professional mentors and the number of female professionals available to mentor is substantial. There will be situations in which female protégés can and will learn a great deal from male mentors. In some situations, male protégés will learn a great deal from female mentors. This is reality. But be aware that it is a potentially dangerous situation and keep careful guard of your heart and your hormones, regardless of your age.

It may not be popular to say so these days, but another advantage of same-gender mentoring is that men understand men and women understand women. Vickie Kraft makes this very point in a section of her book entitled *Women Mentoring Women*:

> There is almost no limit to what women can do today. They can evangelize, teach, serve on church staffs and committees, and be administrators. They can be involved in education at every level, from preschool to graduate school; in children's and youth ministries; in music, art, and drama. They can help the poor and needy in practical ways. Most of all, women can encourage women in this complex and confused society.
>
> Women understand women. We must teach them the

Word so that they know God's standards in order to be equipped for ministry. Then we must encourage them to use their gifts to serve each other and the world around them. It is essential to have women teachers and role models for the generation following us. . . .

There are numerous other reasons women are effective in ministry to women. Who but another woman can fully understand all the differing aspects of pregnancy and childbearing, postpartum blues, and PMS?

Women understand the cabin fever that often attacks in the preschool years that I call "a season of little feet." Another woman understands the weariness and isolation that can result from chasing energetic little ones who communicate primarily in one-syllable words and liberally spread peanut butter and jelly on floors and walls.

An older woman can lift the spirits of a disappointed young wife who is discovering that her knight in shining armor leaves rust spots in the bathroom and socks on the floor. The older woman can help the young wife laugh at her circumstances and can dispel the idea that any knight comes rustproof in a fallen world.

An older woman can encourage her to love and have patience in her marriage. Another woman can share her own life experience in learning how to balance the differing and demanding aspects of managing a home, loving a man, and rearing growing children.[1]

Having a non-Christian Mentor

Scripture is clear that we are not to seek counsel from ungodly people. Psalm 1:1 says, "Blessed in the man who walks not in the counsel of the ungodly." I believe that the value system of a mentor always comes through in a mentoring relationship, and non-Christian value systems spread almost like computer viruses, silently eating away at and corroding our value system. Obviously, being a Christian doesn't guarantee that a person will be a great mentor, but it's a minimum requirement in God's eyes.

However, the Bible does not prohibit godly people from counseling ungodly people. I've reflected many times on the possibility of having non-Christian protégés. I've thought often of helping non-Christians get where they're going, as long as it is moral, ethical, and legal. The possibility of leading that person to a saving faith in Christ over a period of thirty or forty years is exciting.

I suggest that you never have a non-Christian mentor. Seriously consider, however, mentoring a non-Christian protégé. Mentor that person in such a way that over the next five to fifty years, he or she might be attracted to the message of the gospel.

Starting with Unrealistic Expectations

It is easy to develop unrealistic expectations in a mentoring relationship. We live in a dysfunctional society in which protégés may expect that all their troubles will be solved if they find a mentor. This, of course, is not a realistic expectation, but it is common. The person who did not know his father often fantasizes that life would be ideal if he had a fatherly mentor.

An unrealistic expectation of a mentor may be that the protégé will work for the mentor for free. Another is that the mentoring relationship will be that of a parent and child, in which the mentor treats the protégé as a son or daughter. An adult protégé should be treated like an adult friend with whom a mentor shares his or her life experiences.

How to Ensure You Have Realistic Expectations

Dr. Jerry Ballard, a lifelong friend of mine and former president of the World Relief Commission, says, "All miscommunication is the result of differing assumptions." Miscommunication then leads to pressure, frustration, and tension.

If you want to proactively reduce the amount of frustration, pressure, and tension you experience in a mentoring relationship, you must spell out your assumptions as clearly as possible at the outset. Following is an example of a worksheet I recommend you fill out with a prospective mentor or protégé. Your mentoring relationship may be successful without completing this form, but discussing these questions may help you uncover unrealistic expectations that could harm the relationship in the long run. A photocopy-friendly version of this worksheet with lines for writing answers is found in Appendix B.

Clarifying Expectations Before Entering a Mentoring Relationship

1. How much time do the mentor and protégé plan to be together?
2. Will money be loaned?
3. What are the specific needs the protégé feels at this time?

    Imagine that at your first mentor-protégé meeting you discover that the protégé needs to learn how to pole vault, but the mentor has never attended a track meet. As good as the natural chemistry may be, the protégé's expectation is unrealistic unless the mentor has friends in the pole vaulting community.
4. Ideally, how many years do the mentor and protégé expect this relationship to last?
5. Are there any limits the mentor or protégé want to establish?

    Limits and boundaries in a relationship eliminate confusion and apprehension. For instance, a mentor might say, "Call me at any hour in an emergency, but for other questions and conversation, please call between 6 AM and 9 PM." Perhaps a protégé works in a strict environment; he or she might ask the mentor not to call her or him at work to avoid problems.
6. What are the mentor and protégé's assumptions and expectations about the nature of this relationship?
7. Has either the mentor or the protégé experienced failed or disappointing mentoring relationships? Are there any outstanding issues that may have caused

the failure?

8. Do the mentor or protégé expect each other to be perfect? If so, this must be discussed now!

9. What anxieties, uncertainties, uneasiness, and inadequacies does the mentor or protégé feel about this relationship?

A Word about Overcommiting

One final warning: Even if you are excited about mentoring, start with one or two mentoring relationships. Don't get so excited that you overcommit yourself and find it difficult to follow through with your promises. To you, it is simply a busy, jam-packed schedule. To your protégé, it is a broken promise. Start slowly and add protégés as your schedule allows.

Bottom Line

No one can promise you a perfect mentoring relationship! But, you can reduce your risk of a failed mentoring relationship by as much as 80 percent by simply staying within three simple guidelines:

1. Have same-gender mentors and protégés (if possible).
2. Have only Christian mentors.
3. Discuss, and if possible agree on a few basic assumptions as you start your mentoring relationship!

[1]Kraft, Vickie, *Women Mentoring Women: Ways to Start, Maintain, and Expand a Biblical Women's Ministry* (Chicago: Moody Press, 1992), 21.

PART THREE

The Primary Benefits of Having a Mentor

Protégés benefit greatly from having mentors.

There are many professional benefits. Those with mentors have advantages in the workplace. Learning from a mentor's track record of failures and successes allows a protégé to avoid a groping trial-and-error learning process. Ideally, protégés can save time, energy, and money on their way to achieving their professional goals.

There are emotional benefits. Those with mentors have a feeling of security. They know they are not alone on the "Mountain of Life" when life's winds start to blow. A person feels vulnerable without someone, besides family, who cares if he or she lives or dies. A mentor becomes a safety rope in the middle of the night when the protégé feels himself or herself slipping off the mountain.

There are developmental benefits. For many protégés, mentoring is the relationship God uses to help them develop confidence that they have made it to adulthood.

CHAPTER 8

A Head Start in the Workplace: Professional Benefits

Please take sixty seconds right now to ask yourself three simple questions:

1. If one or more people whom you admire a great deal offered themselves and their resources to help you reach your professional goals in the next few years, do you think it would accelerate your progress?

2. If in your workplace, one or more people were mentoring you and you were mentoring one or more people, would you think twice before leaving the organization?

3. If you had one or more mentors, would you be more stable when a crisis occurred? Would you have more confidence, poise, or wisdom?

If you would benefit from having mentors and protégés, so would everyone else on your team! The benefits are very real, especially as the relationships develop over the years. Mentoring relationships increase the rate of organizational growth, reduce turnover, and maintain organizational stability!

Mentoring in a professional setting gives the protégé a major advantage, a tremendous head start, a leg up. It moves a protégé from the trial-and-error process of professional growth to growth built on the track record of the mentor. Instead of experimenting, a protégé has access to experienced wisdom to help make choices. Everything that's not in the manuals—the important stuff—is available to the protégé from his or her mentors.

The Advantages of a Workplace Mentor

Having a business mentor is a widely recognized advantage. Here are a few of the many professional advantages of the mentoring relationships: Assignments are finished quicker, promotions come sooner, and raises are larger. The trip up the ladder is more direct, with fewer "rabbit trails" along the way. Mentoring is typically not what determines if you will be successful in a given assignment. Mentoring simply accelerates the speed with which you will get where you are going!

- With a mentor's objectivity on your side, you are a bit surer that the direction you have chosen is the right one!
- With a mentor's wisdom on your side, you are a bit clearer about your reasons for going in that direction!
- With a mentor's network on your side, you meet the people needed to get you where you are going!

There are many advantages of a workplace mentor!

Mentoring Often Leads to Increased Success

Occasionally, Angelo and Cindy D'Amico invite me to Hilton Head Island to speak at a conference of approximately two thousand entrepreneurial business people. After I spoke at the conference the second year, Angelo, Cindy, their sons Brian and Mark, and I were having lunch. I was trying to summarize my experience with their team, and my bottom line comment was, "This is a great place to grow up, to mature, to have someone who cares help you succeed. What you have here in many of the relationships is basically mentoring."

Angelo's team is built on the premise that the mentor helps the protégé succeed. Thereby, the mentor succeeds even more. Listen to the way Angelo sees it:

> For most of my adult life, I searched for a mentor, someone I could trust, rely upon, and from whom I could seek advice for direction in my life.
>
> Several years ago I got involved with mentoring and have found it to be a most important activity for self-development, and a life-changing experience. It was only through mentoring others as a successful businessman that I really understood why I was doing what I was doing to become successful; I felt like I became a "conscious competent" through mentoring.
>
> It is extremely helpful to focus both on giving to and receiving from others. As the world becomes more high-tech, the need for high-touch becomes more important. Only through nurturing, mentoring relationships will people grow and accomplish their destinies.

Mentoring May Lead to a Major Change in Values

In the mid-1990s, Cheryl and I built a home just north of Orlando, Florida. This was our first experience at building a custom home. Helping us in the process was a longtime friend and world-class design architect, Dennis Kowal.

One afternoon as we were chatting, Dennis shared some of his life story, including the following account of the high impact role Larry Burkett played in shaping his entire value system. I later asked Dennis to write out his story so you could read first-hand how Larry's wisdom and commitment helped shape Dennis over the years.

> Mentoring comes in many shapes and sizes. Mine first came in a UPS carton back in 1987. Just returning from the huge National Religious Broadcasters conference where I sought out a seminar called "Biblical Principles for Operating Your Business," I found myself struggling with a career decision in my field of architecture. On

77

the surface, I had arrived at a comfortable place in life. I had just been made an associate at the firm where I worked, complete with the benefits of a staff to handle the tasks I didn't enjoy doing, autonomy, and a nice pay raise.

I had nearly forgotten the speaker from the seminar, Larry Burkett, a man who got my attention with "there are more verses in the Bible on money and finances than on sex and immorality." But a surprise delivery suddenly got my attention. It was filled with every book and audio tape produced by Larry, who must have kept my business card from our brief meeting after the seminar. God used Larry's gesture because I devoured the materials on how to run a God-glorifying business, and within weeks I quit my job and started my own architectural practice with no clients, no office, and no money. Excited about the remarkable possibility that God was interested in the business world and that I could trust God to operate my business debt free, I experienced a blessed first year with design projects at the Lincoln Center for the Performing Arts in New York City and won clients like the New York Public Library.

When my income neared six figures after the first year, I met with Larry Burkett again to get my next direction. Surely, he would advise me on whether to invest in gold, rare coins, or some promising stocks. Instead, he stunned me with "now you and your wife must pray about setting a lifestyle." He meant that just because the business was financially successful, my salary did not necessarily need to spiral upward with it. It took me only a few months to again see his wisdom as the PTL ministry came crashing down, proving his point that although I earned the money, God may not have intended for me to keep it. This advice would also serve me well through the recession years that laid ahead.

At our yearly meetings, Larry would listen to my eagerness and always have insight. He tempered my intoxication with success by reminding me about my chief purpose in life: to glorify God. He helped me understand my personality type and why I was having so much trouble relating to my secretary and my wife. He also patiently answered the handful of questions I brought to him each year.

As a direct result of his mentoring, I no longer have a "business" but a "ministry" using the vehicle of architecture to reach hurting people with God's message of love. Yes, I am still successfully designing many challenging buildings, but Larry has coached me in the more important realm of building lasting relationships for God. There are many days when God sends people to our office, like an insurance salesman last week, who soon drop their guard and their agenda and melt into their humanness. Sometimes they leave encouraged, sometimes they leave with God's plan of salvation, and sometimes we just cry together.

Thank you Larry, for taking the time to help someone you didn't know to get somewhere we didn't expect.

Mentoring Sometimes Leads to a Lifelong Business Relationship

David Harmon, president of ABC Bank in Lubbock, Texas, may qualify as the world's most gracious person. Several years ago David invited me to come and speak at a business seminar. Later he invited me back to Lubbock to give the keynote address to launch the Lubbock United Way campaign he was chairing.

David and I have become good friends. Each time I visit Lubbock, we take advantage of the time to chat for a few hours about our past, present, and future.

I think it was on my first visit to Lubbock that David told me about his lifelong relationship with his friend Grover Hansen. I was so inspired I asked David to share the story with you.

79

A TRIBUTE TO MY MENTOR, GROVER J. HANSEN
by David M. Harmon, Senior Vice President
Lubbock National Bank

During college I served as vice president of the Association of Student Governments of the United States. I traveled to Chicago from our Washington, D.C., office trying to raise funds for our organization, which encouraged peaceful change through student government during the Vietnam War.

After calling on large corporations for several days in Chicago, I was broke and did not know where I would sleep that night or how I would eat. Chicago, to a young college student from a small Texas town of twenty thousand, was formidable.

On my last call of the day I met Grover J. Hansen, Senior Vice President of First Federal Savings and Loan of Chicago (now Citicorp Savings). Grover started visiting with me while I waited to see the president. He asked tough questions such as, "Where are you staying?" Realizing I had few options, he invited me to his home for dinner where I stayed with him and his family for two weeks. He let me use the vacant board chairman's office to make phone calls and loaned me a secretary for dictating correspondence. He invited me to a weekly prayer breakfast that included presidents of banks and some Fortune 500 companies. He went with me when I addressed the Rotary Club of Chicago and the Illinois Manufacturer's Association.

A few years later Grover Hansen was named president of First Federal. Typical of his kindness was the hospitality he demonstrated by making room reservations at the

Union League Club each time my wife, Rachel, and I visited Chicago.

Looking back at how a total stranger took me in when I was twenty-two years old, I feel a rush of compassion and gratitude. Grover set a standard for me that I will always try to achieve. Grover Hansen is a life-long friend and mentor.

Rothschilding

I heard this story a few years ago. Although I may have embellished and possibly distorted it a bit over the years, I believe it is based in fact. It illustrates exactly the kind of advantage a person has in a professional mentor:

The patriarch of the Rothschild dynasty in old England had an office on what would be the equivalent of the New York Stock Exchange floor. One day, a very enterprising young Englishman approached the elderly gentleman and asked for a loan of five thousand pounds sterling. As he listened carefully, the banking magnet had a twinkle in his eye and excitement in his face that made the young man jump to the conclusion that he would certainly say yes to his rather sizable loan request.

However, at the end of the presentation, the elder Rothschild said, "Young man, I am not going to give you the loan you requested," at which time the young man's heart sank to the floor. He realized that after all the time, hope, energy, and money he had invested in the presentation, he was not going to get the money he desperately needed from the Rothschild family.

"But," the old gentleman continued, "I am going to do something for you that is even more valuable."

Can't you just hear the eager young Englishman, whose body chemistry had just fallen from an adrenaline rush to instant anguish, saying with a bit of cynicism in his mind, "Oh, really? What could be more valuable than five thousand pounds sterling at the time when I need it the most?"

81

The sage Rothschild continued, "Instead of simply giving you five thousand pounds, I will walk with you around the exchange floor. I will introduce you to my friends as my friend. By the time we return to my office, there will be six men who would eagerly loan you five million pounds."

This is a part of professional mentoring I refer to as *Rothschilding*. It may sound unfair to some people, but it is a part of the real business world. In addition to having access to your professional mentor's knowledge and experience, you have the invaluable opportunity to be introduced as your mentor's friend to people who can open up a wide world of business opportunities.

Bottom Line

In many ways a professional mentoring relationship could be likened to gold mining. You never know exactly what you will learn about life, or discover about yourself, on any given day:
- Some days, nothing much seems to happen in the relationship.
- Some days, you find a nugget here and there.
- Some days, you hit the mother lode.

CHAPTER 9

Security on the Mountain of Life: Emotional Benefits

Who in your life actually cares if you live or die?

Who cares enough about how you will finish life to confront you about what you are doing, or are about to do, wrong?

Whom do you care about in the same way?

Welcome to the Mountain of Life

Imagine a picture postcard day. The sky is cloudless. The temperature is perfect. You are feeling on top of the world. You decide to go out to your favorite mountain and climb to the top. Since it's such a nice day, you forget to bring any of your safety gear. But what could go wrong?

You invite a few friends to join you, but no one can make it. You decide to go anyway! You won't be gone long, and what could go wrong?

When you get to the mountain, it is just as you had pictured it. You climb the sheer rock cliffs where your fingers can barely catch the next crevice. Suddenly, your toe slips and you look two thousand feet below you, straight down. You've got no safety lines! You've got no friends, buddies, or mates up there with you. But what could possibly go wrong? Nothing could go wrong today, right?

Soon, the temperature starts to drop, and before you can get more than one hundred feet back down, you see an enormous storm coming over the top of the mountain. In a matter of minutes, you are hanging on to the edge of the cliff—cold, wet, hungry, and alone. The temperature drops further, and ice starts forming on the ledges. Before you know it, darkness sets in. You are now chilled to the bone, alone, hanging on the side of a mountain with no safety lines, in the middle of the night. There is no one to hear if you fall!

This picture is an emotional analogy of many people I have talked with in the past twenty years. This is how many people feel a high percentage of the time. They feel totally alone to deal with life's threats. They feel like they are on a ledge, and taking the wrong step could lead to ruin. There's no phone number to call to say, "I need help!" There is no safety line. There is no other human being to whom they can confidently and confidentially turn for help.

When you are on the "mountain of life" alone, you need a prayer life in good working order and a mentor. When your protégé is up there on the mountain of life alone in the middle of a storm, you are desperately needed on the next ledge up. Here is where you, as the mentor, stand with a safety rope. In case your protégé falls, you're there to hold her or him to the hill. If, because of your protégé's weight, you begin to feel the bone-numbing strain and your fingers begin to lose their strength, you need a mentor above you, holding you with a safety cord.

Now imagine for a minute this same mountain of life with about three hundred climbers strung up along the hill, all tied by safety lines to each other. You are your protégé's mentor, but someone else is your mentor, and someone else is your mentor's mentor. You teach your protégé, "Don't only be mentored. There are young kids coming up, your sister or brother in junior high school, or your cousin in college. Lock on to them. Be their mentor." On the mountain of life, you don't have to be alone. You've got other Christian brothers and sisters, other mentors, and other protégés, so if you slip, you don't fall two thousand feet.

Everyone needs a few committed friends with a safety-line network in life; people to protect you from making drastic mistakes; people to keep you on the mountain and help you to a safer ledge.

"Sit Down!"

Let me tell you a true story about when I desperately needed someone on the end of the rope or I would have "wiped out on the rocks two thousand feet below!"

Did you ever watch *Happy Days* on television? You remember the Fonz, right? When I was fourteen or fifteen years old in 1958, I was actually living *Happy Days* before the TV sitcom was ever conceived. I knew the person who could have been the prototype of the Fonz. He was my cousin, Bob Batterbee.

Bob Batterbee was something else! He had the ducktail haircut. He had the cool lines, the cool clothes, the cool shoes, the cool girls. He snapped his fingers, and the jukebox started playing cool music!

On the other hand, I was the prototypical Chachi. I was the little cousin he was always trying to teach how to be cool. He was my mentor. He'd say, "When it comes to girls, do this. Don't do that. Always keep your shoes spit shined. Always walk with this cool step—watch me." It was practical stuff for a high school freshman to be learning from his cool cousin in the tenth grade.

One of the lessons Bob Batterbee taught me was simple. He said, "Robert, don't ever talk about fighting. Chickens, wimps, and girls talk about fighting. If somebody's after you, or someone is mouthing off to you, either turn around and walk away and don't care what in the world he thinks about you, or get him looking off somewhere, smack him in the face, and then try to knock his lights out. But don't ever talk about fighting." Bob taught me many things, and I am seriously thankful for all of the time he invested in my life. Today, we remain the best of friends.

Now let's fast forward ten years. I was twenty-four years old, out of graduate school, and married, with a baby, Kimberly. Like most young marriages, ours had its ups and downs. During one of the downs in our marriage I got a call from one of my life mentors, a man named Bill Bullard.

I met Bill while attending Michigan State. We became friends even though he was ten or fifteen years older than me. Now understand, we never used the word *mentor* to describe our relationship. But since I finished graduate school at Michigan State University in 1966, he's called me two or three times a year, just calling to check in. Bill is not related to me, but the day Bill dies I will weep. You know what else? If I die before he does, I think he will weep for me. We have become lifelong friends.

I hadn't seen Bill personally for the year and a half since I left graduate school. So it surprised me somewhat when, at a troubled time in our marriage, he just "happened to call" and say, "Hey, Bobb, just calling to check in. How is everything?"

I said, "Not so good, Bill." His next question was logical enough! "What's wrong?" "Well, you know, Cheryl and I are, you know, not getting along too well," I confessed. He said, "I'll be right down," and he hung up.

Now this was before mobile phones. Bill was in Ann Arbor, Michigan, 185 miles away from South Bend, Indiana, where Cheryl and I were living at the time. I wanted to say, "Don't come, Bill! I'm embarrassed because Cheryl's going to be upset with me for telling you this!" But before I could say, "Don't come," he had already hung up and was on his way!

I had to tell Cheryl. When I did, her response was, "I don't want him to come! Why is he coming?" I sheepishly admitted, "Well I don't want him to come either, but he's coming anyway. I told him we weren't getting along so well."

Bill arrived about four hours later. The three of us talked until two in the morning. He was trying to get a twenty-four-year-old protégé to understand life. Around 2:00 AM, I remembered Bob's counsel: Don't talk about fighting; either fight or walk away. I decided that I'd had enough talking about marriage, or anything else. I got up to leave! I wasn't just leaving the room; I was leaving my wife and my baby.

Bill asked, "Where are you going, Bobb?" I said, "I'm out of here. I'm done talking. No more talking. This is it. I'm done." He said, "Well, where are you going?" I said, "I'm just going. I'm out of here. This marriage is over!"

He said, "Sit down, Bobb." I just stood there looking at him. He could see I hadn't heard, or wasn't listening, so he played the role of a drill-sergeant-mentor and literally shouted, "Bobb, sit down!" I sat down. That was about 1967. Cheryl and I are still happily married and growing in our relationship.

There are many stories I could tell about how Bill has helped over the years as a friend, advisor, sounding board, ride in the middle of the night, place to stay whenever I was in his city—in short—as a mentor.

Since then, I have spoken at several seminars when Bill was in the room. He not only knew when to tell me to sit down; he always tells me he's proud I'm standing up. Thanks again, Bill!

Zingo

Let me tell you a short story about one of my college classmates. I won't tell you his name for soon-to-be-obvious reasons. Let's call him Zingo.

When I first went to Bethel College in Mishawaka, Indiana, at seventeen, I think I may have still had manure under my shoes. Many of my relatives were, and still are, hard-working, successful turkey farmers in Mancelona, Michigan.

As a seventeen-year-old in college, I often felt like a turkey-farm kid—a hayseed, a small village kid, a greenhorn. But there was a student at Bethel named Zingo, and Zingo was a "hot rod." Oh man, was he slick! He wasn't a con man. He was just smooth. He was articulate. He could hold an audience spellbound. When I heard him, I was not only spellbound, but I believed he believed every word he said.

Zingo was nineteen. I thought he would surely be the next Billy Graham. I wasn't the only one who thought so. He was the national preacher boy contest winner at Youth for Christ one year. Any reasonable person watching a hayseed kid from Mancelona, Michigan, having a Coke with this silver-tongued orator would have rated the chances about one thousand to one in the orator's favor to be the one writing the book you are reading.

Zingo married his college sweetheart when he left school, and they had two children. But around age twenty-four, he actually did walk out on his wife, leaving her and the children behind. To the best of my knowledge he has left the faith and has little or no interest in the things of God today.

One of the reasons he fell off the mountain of life, from my perspective, is that he had no mentor at the other end of the rope. He had no one to tell him to sit down. He had no mentor to tell him he was proud that he was standing up. He didn't have anyone who cared enough to help or confront him. So he just walked out.

Mentors Show the Way

Mentors show us where and how to find a safe place to get a toehold or a handhold on the mountain of life. More often than not, a simple "cup of coffee" conversation makes a huge difference when a person is making a critical decision.

- At key decision points the difference between a person staying in a position or resigning is frequently one short conversation with a mentor.
- At turning points of all kinds—job change, birth of a child, death in the family, new assignments—one short conversation with a mentor makes all the difference.
- At points where a protégé has gotten off the track—any kind of financial, moral, ethical, or legal breakdown—one short conversation with a mentor turns the tide.

Otto B. Melby is chairman of the board of Awana Clubs International, one of my clients. One day Otto told me about his early years. He was off the track, and his mentor, Art Rorheim, took the time to care:

> I didn't know it at the time, but God placed a mentor in my life at a very young age! I was a proud twelve-year-old member of the Awana Pioneers club when I met Art Rorheim, the Commander. I wanted to be around him. He was my hero.
>
> But then, just one year later, my dad died. I was devastated! How could God do this to me just when I needed Dad the most?
>
> I began to tag along with older guys. I quickly replaced club friends with boozing buddies. I turned my back on God, and I stayed away from Art. I got into a lot of trouble. At her wit's end, my Mom called Art. He

came over to the house, sat on my bed, and talked to me, reminding me that I would never be happy unless I committed my life to the Lord. I didn't want to hear that. Why should I turn back to God when He turned His back on me?

Art kept caring, visiting, talking, and encouraging. He took me under his wing, and in order to keep me off the streets, he put me to work after school running off Awana handbooks on the mimeograph machine. I saw a consistency in Art's life. He took time. He kept on caring. At a time when I needed a dad, Art was there.

Now that the Lord has brought me back to himself, I look at Art as my earthly spiritual father and know he placed an anchor within my life that kept me from floating too far downstream. He prayed for me all my life. Who knows where I'd be if it weren't for Art? I'd like to say to him: Thanks for praying and for being there when I needed you the most, and thanks for still being there.

A TRIBUTE TO MY MENTORS
By Bill Bullard
Released Friend

Lorne and Lucille Sanny who, during the early days of my walk with Jesus, patiently took me into their home where loving care and discipline could become a part of my life.

Mark Hatfield, the dean of students and professor of political science at Willamette University. Mark took a chance on a low D-average high-school student who had served in the Navy and needed a break to enter college. Providing that break opened the door to my intellectual "conversion," which was second in importance only to my introduction to Jesus of Nazareth. For me, Mark's personal and public life has been a model of independent thinking and integrity.

Abraham Vereide and Dick Halverson, whose walk with people in positions of leadership around the world provided me with a greater sensitivity to other cultures and world issues. Their lives represent commitment for the sake of others and not for the sake of their own institutions or organizations. These two men accepted people where they were and then gently introduced them to Jesus of Nazareth. They have had so much influence around the world through one simple message: "Jesus brings with Him the hope of all the glorious things to come." This has been their legacy in my life.

Bob and Joan Higbee, whose entrance into Wilma's and my life saved our marriage on more than one occasion. As newlyweds in 1957, all four of us needed each other and have continued that caregiving throughout our lives.

In the process of developing leaders, it is just as critical to *keep* the young leaders on the track as it is to get them on the track in the first place. With a wise mentor's counsel, a protégé makes the right choice. Without a wise mentor's counsel, often a protégé makes a short-sighted, unwise, ungodly, wrong choice. Mentors show the way.

Bottom Line

The basic difference between a turkey-farm kid from Mancelona, Michigan, and Zingo? A mountain-of-life mentor at age twenty-four—and beyond!

CHAPTER 10

The Bridge into Adulthood: Developmental Benefits

More so now than ever before, growing up is not easy. Everyone has a unique series of struggles moving from being a junior-high or high-school kid to being a responsible, healthy adult. Sometimes it isn't clear how to get from here to there.

Where did *you* go to learn to be an adult? Where did you go to find healthy role models, healthy attitudes to emulate in adults you could look up to and become like? Where did you go to find someone to know you well enough to help you define your strengths? Where *do* kids go to learn to become adults?

There are no becoming-an-adult schools. There is no authoritative book that tells how to complete the process, but there are mentors. One of the best places to go in the pursuit of adulthood is into a mature mentoring relationship.

The Respect of an Authority Figure

The "formula" is simple but profound: To become an adult—to enter manhood or womanhood—a deeply respected authority figure (a mentor, a parent, an aunt, an uncle, a friend) must accept and respect you as an equal adult.

This adult doesn't see you any longer as a child or as a kid but instead sees you as a mature person who is worthy of adult respect. The mentoring relationship provides a context for such respect to be earned and expressed.

Dr. Jay Kesler, former president of Taylor University, and former president of Youth for Christ, has been my friend for many years and has been a mentor to many. Listen to the story of how mentors have been a part of shaping him into adulthood over the years:

> Dr. Milo Rediger, dean of Taylor University when I was a student, perhaps recognized in me some sense of a combination of intellectual capacity and Christian commitment. He gave me inordinate amounts of his time to work through my process.
>
> One day after class I followed him all the way to the front door of his house, talking. He was totally focused on answering my questions about foreknowledge and predestination. I remember his attention to me was so great that his wife had to literally drag him through the front door to eat his meal. Though he had walked home almost automatically and involuntarily, I believe he forgot he was on his front porch.
>
> I never forgot that and have attempted to give that kind of empathetic listening to young persons who contact me over the years.
>
> Sam Wolgemuth, former president of Youth for Christ, was another mentor who treated me as an adult. Sam never gave me advice of any kind; he simply lived his life in front of me and allowed me to be with him, at his sleeve, attending hundreds and hundreds of meetings where I was able to be a mouse listening in to big people's conversations, as it were. By being allowed to be in the room and never excluding me, he gave me exposure levels to leadership at the top that very few men have ever had.
>
> Though our lives are separated by twenty years, I never felt inferior. I always felt like a little brother or peer in meetings. In Sam's case it was giving me hundreds of hours of his time, driving me, going places with me, sharing with me his feelings and opinions on issues and then living out what he said.

These stories are a classic case study of how a person learns what it means to be an adult and accepts himself or herself as an adult by being respected as one by a mentor.

The Importance of Self-Concept

Another step in reaching adult maturity that is aided by the mentoring relationship is the definition of one's self-concept. Self-concept is a psychological term that I define loosely as "the sum total of all the adjectives you use to describe yourself, both positive and negative." Many times, people's self-concept, self esteem, and self-worth are low because the adjectives they use to describe themselves are mostly negative. They may have a list of three or four positives and thirty or forty negatives.

When a protégé has a poor self-concept, a mentor can begin questioning the negative adjectives (such as *sloppy, undisciplined,* and *procrastinating*) and reinforcing the positive adjectives (such as *neat, disciplined,* and *action-oriented*) so that the protégé's self concept becomes progressively more positive, healthier, stronger, and clearer.

Personal growth is one of the most frequent results of the mentoring relationship. I define personal growth as "turning negative adjectives into positive ones." The protégé might say, "I used to see myself as a procrastinator. Now I see myself as an action-oriented person." That's personal growth, and it is encouraged as the mentor helps the protégé define and identify strengths that he or she has not seen before and grow past some of the negatives.

A large part of growing into adulthood is simply having a mentor who cares enough to help us define our strengths, our growth areas, and help us develop a bridge of personal growth as we make the transition from child to adult.

The Manhood Struggle

A male mentor is often a surrogate dad, a father figure, or a mature model of genuine manhood. The mentor is frequently the person who helps a protégé enter manhood by accepting the protégé as an equal adult!

93

Almost one-third of the men I work with in a small group setting say they have struggled all their life with questions such as: What is a man? When does a man become a man? How does a man become a man? Am I a man?

I believe one of the reasons that mentoring is important today is that men have moved away from their uncles—the men who typically affirm a man's manhood. One of the roles of the mentoring relationship is providing that affirmation.

Late one evening I was watching a well-known interviewer of TV celebrities interview one of Hollywood's hottest macho men at the time.

The interviewer's questions probed below the surface: "You're a man's man. You're a macho man. When does a man become a man?"

The star reflected for what seemed like a long time, maybe as much as fifteen- to thirty-seconds of dead-air silence. Then he smiled the mustache-covered smile he is famous for and replied, "A man becomes a man when his daddy tells him he is, and not until." And I thought, *Well, you old fox. That was a far smarter and more serious answer than I expected from you.*

It took about three months for that little commentary to explode like a bomb in my brain. I thought, *Oh, no! If that's the case, we're in deeper weeds than I thought!* Many fathers died or left when their sons were very young. Other fathers were unsure in their own manhood. Imagine asking your father, "Am I a man?" and having your dad say, "I don't know. I don't know if I am a man! Who am I to say if *you* are or not?"

If our dads do not tell us, for whatever reason, that we are men, the most logical assumption is that an uncle will assume that position. He might say, "You know, you are really becoming an adult. Come to the Good Old Boys Club, or come to the Rotary with me, or come on this fishing trip with the men," or something else to let us know that he accepts us as a man. But I mentioned earlier, we frequently live hundreds of miles from our uncles. Our uncles often really don't even know us. Some dads, and some uncles, are divorced, in broken relationships, or emotionally immature. They're struggling with manhood issues themselves again!

A woman can make a man feel like a man sexually. But as I have listened to men struggle with manhood, I have concluded that a woman alone cannot affirm a man's manhood. Only being accepted as an equal by another man can. If the father or uncles are unavailable, that leaves a mentor. Mentoring is one entry way to becoming a man.

A TRIBUTE TO JOSH MCDOWELL
By Dan Hitzhusen, Church Planter
Global Missions Fellowship

Josh saw me as a diamond in the rough. I was twenty-one years old with a heart for God, full of life, and full of myself. Serving as a personal assistant to Josh McDowell as a staff member of Campus Crusade for Christ, I made many mistakes. Josh expected excellence, yet, when I blew it, he would say something like, "Dan, that just shows it can happen to the best of them."

I remember really messing something up and asking Josh why he didn't get particularly angry with me. He said, "Dan, the things that I think will make you a better person, a better friend, a better representative of Jesus Christ, I share with you. Everything else I take to God."

On another occasion, I was feeling rejected by some of my coworkers. Josh pulled me aside and said, "Dan, you and I are renegades. We are different. We will never really fit in. You will never fit in. That isn't the way God made you."

Josh always believed in me more than I believed in myself

Perhaps the greatest personal tribute that I have for Josh McDowell is that he saw me for who God made me to be and he encouraged me to serve God with my whole heart in my own uniqueness.

Again, this is why the mentoring relationship holds such promise for so many men. It is a relationship in which one's manhood can be affirmed by another respected, mature man.

During a Promise Keepers' rally in 1993, Howard Hendricks told this story:

> A few weeks ago my wife and I were in Jerusalem. We were at the Wailing Wall. We counted five bar mitzvahs. It was the most exciting thing in my trip to Israel, to watch these boys taken by a father, taken by an uncle, taken by a friend, hoisted to their shoulders, danced around that sacred area with people clapping and singing and women throwing candy.
>
> I turned to my wife and said, "Sweetheart, those boys will never forget this day!" What do we have in American society that even partially replicates that?
>
> Someone asked me in a television interview recently, "What would you say has been your greatest contribution as a seminary professor?" I said, "To affirm the maleness of many of my students."

One other point, before we leave the father, son, mentor topic. Literally millions of men have never heard their father say two of the most meaningful phrases in the English language: "I love you" and "I'm proud of you!"

Tragically, many never will. Perhaps the father has passed away. In many cases they are alive but unable to communicate in emotionally significant ways. They are emotionally stoic or in some situations so needy themselves it never occurs to them to try to meet the needs of their sons.

Enter the mentor! If you are a mentor, you are likely the single most positive cheerleader your protégé has ever had. Your "I'm proud of you! You are going to make it! You're okay! I love you!" may well be the highlight of your male protégé's year.

The Womanhood Struggle

The most typical heart-cry I hear from women is, "My mother won't let me grow up. She treats me like a child. She can't accept the fact that I am a mature, adult woman."

One of the most desperate needs in society is for mature women who will become mentors. Of course, younger women need experienced, mature adult women to help them learn to cook, grow professionally, raise children, and relate to a husband. But what is crucially needed are experienced women who will treat a female protégé as an adult equal, as a grown-up, as a peer, and as a friend. When this happens, the protégé will finally feel she's become an adult woman.

A common problem related to women in the mentoring relationship is the generational gap between homemakers and professional women. A few decades ago, the majority of women saw their role as homemakers, not professional women. Today, the majority of women graduating from college and going into various professions see themselves as professional women. Frequently they do not have role models within their families to help them, to mentor them in their roles as professional women. There is a tremendous need for Christian professional women to be mentors for young women.

It is heartbreaking to ask, "What woman do you, as a young, professional, Christian woman, admire or respect the most in your profession or in your area of expertise?" and be told, "I don't know any other Christian woman in my profession, let alone one that I admire or respect."

The following was originally recorded for the national radio series *Focus on the Family*, featuring psychologist and best-selling author, Dr. James Dobson, and a panel of women including Vickie Kraft, author of *Women Mentoring Women*:

Woman to Woman

Dobson: What worries you all the most about the younger generation of women coming up today? If you had to make a commentary on what it means to be a woman in Western society today, and what aspect of that is the most risky, and the most dangerous, what would you say?

Panel: I worry most that they will not value themselves as unique creations of God. I do believe that God created man and woman. He did not create one thing. He created two separate sexes for specific reasons.

Dobson: All right, what does that really mean now? We've got a very bright young lady. She's twenty-five years old, married. She has this brilliant law career ahead of her, and the question of raising a child comes up, and whether intentionally or not, she gets pregnant. She has the baby. Now the child is one year of age, and there is a definite conflict with her career. Talk to her.

Vickie: Well, she just has to realize that some things are more important than others, and that baby will never be one year old again, and that baby needs its mother now. The law career, she can keep up with courses, she can keep up with magazines, she can keep up, she can go back for refresher courses. There will always be lawyers, but there will never again be a mother for that child that can take her place. *She* is the mother of that child. And it's a matter of priorities, that's all. And we're not saying, "Don't be a lawyer!" We're saying, "Put this on hold." That's all. All of us have done that!

Dobson: Gail, does that make sense to your generation? You graduated from the University of Texas. You have a seven-year-old daughter. Is there a thumb in your back to get out and use the mind that you have? You are very

---

bright. You were at the top of your class. What kind of pressure is on you?

Gail: Because I surround myself with Christian women primarily, I don't feel the kind of pressure that I would if I were not in women's ministries. But I do see within my neighborhood, within the business world, and with other clubs I'm in that are charity-based, that there is that devaluing of the role of being a mother. They don't understand the intellectual development of their children, the emotional development, the physical development. They have learned about everything else, but they are woefully unprepared to be mothers, and not until the kids get into high school do you start seeing them sometimes realizing that they've made some serious, serious errors, and they wish that they could turn the clock back, but they can't,

Dobson: Do you think society is beginning to recognize that? Do you think there is a movement?

Gail: I think that they are beginning to because there are women in their thirties and forties, especially in their forties, that are now saying, "It hasn't worked! Look at our high schools right now, and all the discipline problems we now have!" But I'm concerned that even with young Christian women, that they feel that pull that to have value they must have a job as well. Sometimes we see even husbands tell them that they don't have an option, that they have to work, and the husbands are not even seeing the value of what they are doing! Now I realize that there are some women who must work, and there are creative ways that they may be able to find work in the home, or to find an aunt, or a grandmother, or a caring, nurturing woman to help in that area.

Vickie: We're not talking about the single mother who is divorced, didn't want to be, or widowed, or something. That's a different situation.

Bottom Line

The mentoring relationship is a pathway, a bridge, a process, that allows many protégés to grow into mature adulthood.

PART FOUR

A Protégé's Perspective

Every protégé feels a bit nervous, eager, anxious, excited, uneasy, and a wide variety of other emotions at the very thought of having someone they deeply respect as a mentor. No protégé has ever wanted to fail as a protégé. Every single one wants to do it right; to look, seem, and be just what they are to be as a protégé. But what does it mean to be a protégé? How does one go about it? What do you say, do, and how do you behave? How do you get started? In the following chapters you will find my very best thoughts on the subject.

What to Look for
in a Mentor

I have worked with a lot of protégés who have had all the potential in the world. They were brilliant, eager, teachable, and friendly. They had bright futures, appreciative attitudes, and all of the dimensions you could want in a protégé, but they had a lot of fear in their hearts about approaching a mentor to explore a mentoring relationship.

Heart-Fears about Looking for a Mentor

The most common fears I hear are, "Why would this person want to put up with me, or want to help me? Would this person reject me? Would I look like too big a failure to this person if they knew the real me? Would they want to control me?" All of these heart-fears can come popping into your emotions when you are thinking about approaching a mentor.

The questions often continue as potential protégés consider actually asking someone to be their mentor. "Will I look awkward? Will I look like a fool? Will I blow it? Will I say the wrong thing? Will I do the wrong thing? Will I ask too much? Will I ask the wrong thing?"

One of the ways to begin to get rid of the fears is to get a clear idea of exactly what you are looking for in a mentor. Hopefully, the following checklist will help.

The "Ideal Mentor" Checklist

The following checklist is a rather detailed, point by point, academic exercise to help you find the ideal mentor for you. This checklist is only an attempt to help bring clarity in defining the kind of person for whom you are looking.

But even before you start reading this checklist, let me suggest that what you're really looking for is a person that you know cares for you, believes in you, and naturally encourages you. A good mentor is a person you enjoy being with, who has more experience than you have, and who would be happy to help you win in life. If you already have that person in mind, this checklist will only confirm your intuitive guess that this person would make a great mentor.

The checklist is also helpful if you have two or three mentors to consider, but cannot determine which one you will ask. The mentoring checklist can bring out a few fine points that may help you make your final decision.

Before you choose a mentor, check to see if he or she has these qualities:

Your Ideal Mentor Is...

1. Honest With You

For example, one of my male protégés was very much a man but he had effeminate gestures. When the time was right, after several hours of talking about a wide variety of topics, I decided the time had come to be dangerously candid. I actually had to teach this friend how to use his hands and his head. That's an example of raw honesty that was objective enough to help the protégé see clearly his potential and also the roadblocks keeping him from that potential. It's a little like being a loving uncle or aunt, someone who will take you aside on occasion and tell you things you need to hear but frankly don't necessarily want to hear.

2. A Model for You

Thomas Carlyle's words are worth repeating: "Be what you would have your pupils to be." When I take my associate team along for client consultations, I ask them, "What did you learn by watching me as well as by listening to me?" Part of your mentor's role is teaching you by letting you watch him or her, in addition to telling you things.

3. Deeply Committed to You

It may be a little difficult to see a mentor or a protégé as family. The apostle Paul, when writing to his young protégé, Timothy, captured this thought when he said, "Do not rebuke an older man, but exhort him as a father, younger men as brothers, older women as mothers, younger women as sisters, with all purity" (1 Tim. 5:1, NKJV). Even though they are probably not blood relatives, see both your mentor and your protégé with a family level of commitment.

4. Open and Transparent

Cheryl, my wife, often encourages me, "Your associate team only hears about your successes. Let them hear also about your failures." I have to watch very carefully that I tell my associate team not only when I have won, but also when I have lost and feel like a failure. For example, my associates often get the false impression that I am always "feeling like I'm on top of the world" because I am typically "up" when I'm with them. When they learned I have several days a year when I am deeply discouraged and feel depressed, they realized that being a consultant wasn't only for "super positive" people, but regular human beings as well.

Every mentor has struggles that the protégé never sees. The protégé might say with some hesitation, "My mentor can do this, but I don't know if I'll ever make it because I have problems with discipline (or doubt, or self-worth, or fatigue)." Ask your mentor to share her or his struggles along with the success stories she or he is trying to teach.

5. A Teacher

Many people do things well, but don't know how to tell another person how they did it. At one time they learned how to do a given exercise (an accounting practice, a writing style, a trick of the trade) but have long since forgotten how they do it. Look for a mentor that can tell you how and why he or she did or didn't do something.

6. One Who Believes in Your Potential

My father-in-law, Joe Kimbel, is one of my life mentors. Once he introduced me to his friends by saying, "I'd like to have you meet my son-in-law, Bobb Biehl." Then he added, "Some day they'll say, "I'd like to have you meet Joe Kimbel, Bobb Biehl's father-in-law." That very thing happened twenty years later in Orlando, Florida, and I was humbled when I recalled his gracious prediction.

Your ideal mentor needs to be the kind of person who looks at you and says, "Yes, I think this person has tremendous potential. I think if I invest some of my life in this person, he or she has what it takes to make a real difference." Surprisingly, most Christian leaders with whom I have worked say they have never had a single person say to them, "You are a leader!"

7. One Who Can Help You Define Your Dream and a Plan to Turn Your Dream into Reality

Ideally, you are looking for a mentor who can help you clarify things which are in your head and in your heart. The mentor helps you answer the "dream question": "How can I make the most significant difference for God in my lifetime?"

Once clear, the ideal mentor can help you decide which of these dreams seem realistic and which do not.

a. You may feel like you have tremendous potential but won't allow yourself to believe in yourself. You may place unrealistic limits on yourself that the mentor has to help you eliminate. A mentor can help you see potential, even though you might not yet see it. They see greater ability in you than you see in yourself. Then they tell you to "Go for it!"

b. You may have an over-inflated evaluation of your capabilities in a given area. It is your mentor who may need to help you see that you can't carry a tune, and should start thinking about a few options if your aspiration of being a star at the Metropolitan Opera doesn't work out.

Note: Just because your mentor says you can or cannot achieve something doesn't necessarily make it so. Your mentor is simply a human being trying her or his very best to help you. Take her or his input seriously. But the final decision, and responsibility, of the direction of your life obviously rests with you. Mentors are just there to help.

Once the realism factor has been established, he or she can help you develop a plan to move from where you are to where you ultimately dream of being.

8. Successful in Your Eyes

You must feel that your mentor is the kind of person you would like to be like some day, in some ways.

9. Open to Learning from You, As Well As Teaching You

This might sound odd as a prerequisite for being a good mentor because it seems like the mentor's job to teach and the protégé's job to learn. But I have found that if I remain teachable, then I am modeling the teachability which I want my protégé to have. You can learn from everyone. What's more, I have found that as a mentor pours himself into a person and gives and gives and gives, sooner or later that person in whom he has invested so much will want to give something back.

As I mentioned earlier, Ross Goebel was one of my protégés. Over the years we have spent days in deep conversation about some aspect of his life or future. At the same time, Ross, a computer genius, has spent a lot of time teaching me the newest ways to make my laptop behave. I taught and learned. He taught and learned.

Let's say I, as your mentor, have a whole sack of oranges. You're thirsty and I give you some of my oranges. Sooner or later you'll want to give something back to me. You might say, "How about a tangerine from me?" If I say, "No, no thank you," that makes it seem as though what I give is valuable but what you give is not. It shuts off the chemistry. If

109

I, the mentor, can learn from you, then suddenly mentoring becomes a two-way street. You think to yourself, *Hey, my mentor respects me* (and vice versa).

10. Willing to Stay Primarily on Your Agenda, Not Her or His Own

This is part of the definition of the mentoring relationship.

Conclusion

A mentor is a person who believes in you and wants to see you win. If you can stay with these items and make certain that this is what your mentor will bring to the relationship, you will find that the relationship will get off on the right foot. If you don't have any of these, there is a high likelihood that the relationship may be less satisfying to both of you.

On the chart on the following page you can:
- evaluate current mentors
- compare future mentors
- identify what is missing in any given mentor

Bottom Line

In all of your analysis, be careful not to forget the simple truth that what you're really looking for is a person that you know cares for you, believes in you, and encourages you. A good mentor is a person that you naturally enjoy being with, that has more experience than you have, that would be happy to help you win in life, to help you grow in sensitive areas most other friends simply "put up with" on a day to day basis. If you have found this person, you have found a mentor.

Mentor's Profile	Mentor One	Mentor Two	Mentor Three
1. Honest with you			
2. A model for you			
3. Deeply committed to you			
4. Open and transparent			
5. A teacher			
6. One who believes in your potential			
7. One who can help you define your dream and a plan to turn your dream into reality			
8. Successful in your eyes			
9. Open to learning from you, as well as teaching you			
10. Willing to stay primarily on your agenda, not his/her own			

CHAPTER 12

Finding and Approaching a Mentor

I want to make the process of actually finding and approaching a mentor as easy as possible. The following checklist gives you a step-by-step way to incorporate ideas in previous chapters. It may prove most valuable in increasing your confidence by making the way clear.

As you begin the process, remember your future mentor will be as happy to have you as a protégé as you will be to have her or him as a mentor.

Checklist for Selecting and Approaching a Mentor

1. Define the essence of what you need from a mentor.

> I did this in the last chapter when I said you're looking for a person who cares for you, believes in you, and encourages you. Perhaps you have ideas to add. You may even want to express what you need in altogether different terms.

2. Review ideal mentor checklist.

> Do this before you begin to think of candidates as well as after you have some people in mind. It will give you a good foundation throughout the process and will increase your ability to make a thoughtful choice.

3. Make a list of the top three mentor candidates.

Of all the people you know and respect, which three would you most like to have as life mentors? Write their names here:

1. _____

2. _____

3. _____

I ask you to list three because I recommend that you start with one to three mentors. You may eventually have several mentors, each helping you in a different area of your life (for example, one spiritual, one professional, and one social).

You are not limited to looking for one mentor for all aspects of life. Often it makes more sense to look for people who can help you in specific areas.

4. Review the definition of mentoring to see which of the three candidates seems to fit best.

Mentoring is a lifelong relationship in which a mentor helps a protégé reach her or his God-given potential.

5. Ask God to make His will clear.

I advise that you ask God to make clear who He wants to be your mentors. Don't forget the warning of Psalm 1:1: "Blessed is the man who walks not in the counsel of the ungodly" (NKJV).

6. Meet with the potential mentor.

Once you have selected a potential mentor, in your own way and time approach that person and say something like this: "I would like for you to consider being one of my life mentors.

What I mean by that is simple:

- I'd like to be on your lifelong prayer list.
- Every time we meet, I'll come prepared with specific priorities and tell you exactly the help or advice I need.
- Bottom line: I need help from a mature person like you to realize my full God-given potential over a lifetime."

7. Once agreed, review assumptions (see chapter 7).

If the person agrees, be a great protégé! (The next chapter will give you some ideas.) Start by discussing your and your new mentor's assumptions to avoid unrealistic expectations. If the person declines, don't get discouraged. Just pull out your list of potential mentors (you should have at least two other names) and go to step 4 of this checklist. If necessary, start over at step 3 or even step 1, but stay positive and stay on track. You will find the mentor who is right for you.

Bottom Line

In seeking a mentor, don't hesitate—initiate!

CHAPTER 13

How to be a Great Protégé

You know by now that I am excited about mentoring. In my excitement, I could create a complicated, detailed, overwhelming list of fifty or even one hundred qualities that the perfect protégé should have.

Instead, I want to share with you the very best of what I know about being a great protégé. There are four things you can do to make a drastic difference in your mentor's eagerness to get together with you. If you take them to heart, these four little verbs will help your mentor to look forward to helping you.

1. Admire

When I say admire, I mean *show* it. I'm not advocating flattery, but feelings of admiration for your mentor. If you are thinking something like: *This is helpful. How do you know all this? I'm amazed. Wow!*, say it to your mentor. When you express how helpful your mentor has been, or how genuinely amazed you are at your mentor, he or she will want to share more and more with you.

2. Appreciate

Expressing your appreciation is also crucial. When you sincerely feel it, say, "Thank you, that really helped. It will make a big difference. It may change my whole life." Words like these fuel your mentor's willingness to help you. Your mentor is not supporting you for money or glory, but a grateful word from you will mean a lot.

3. Consider

It is only fair that you be considerate of your mentor. Make it as convenient as possible for your mentor to help you. I'm talking about extremely practical consideration. For example say, "I'll drive over to your place. I'll pick you up. Whatever is best for your schedule."

4. Love

I hope you have chosen a mentor you genuinely like and enjoy being with and look forward to giving back to, becoming a lifelong friend with, and staying with over many years. Your mentor cares for you and helps you and should never be viewed as simply a boost to the next rung on the corporate ladder. It is natural to develop love for your mentor and very wise to express it from time to time.

Bottom Line

If you truly like your mentor and enjoy being with her or him, your mentor will sense that and will receive tremendous pleasure from the relationship.

So express your admiration, appreciation, and love for your mentor. In doing so, you will make it easy for him or her to help you.

CHAPTER 14

Thanking Mentors

I want to elaborate on the theme of showing appreciation to mentors, which I brought up in chapter 13. In your lifetime, there has likely been someone who made an emotional commitment to you, and you felt their strength for years. They may never have said, "I'd like to be your mentor," but you've known they were in your corner.

All too often, we forget to adequately thank the very people who have helped us the most. For example, Alene Neeland, one of the two teachers in my entire academic career who I felt cared personally for me, died before I had a chance to tell her how much she meant to me.

I don't want you to miss an opportunity. Stop right now and think of up to five people who have significantly influenced your life. They can be your formal or your informal mentors. Seriously consider dropping them a note of thanks, putting in your own words one or more of the following thoughts:

- I am reading a book on mentoring, and even though we've never mentioned that you are my mentor in a formal way, I want you to know that I appreciate the fact that you have cared for me over the years.

- I'll never forget the day you taught me to _____.

I felt so nervous, so insecure, and so inadequate. Knowing that you were there and that you believed I could do it made all the difference in the world.

- You'll never know how much your belief in me has caused me to believe in myself.

- The day you helped me _____ is a day I'll never forget. As long as I live, I'll appreciate the way you helped me get through that day.

- I'll never forget when I was so discouraged, depressed, and despondent. When we got together and you told me _____, that snapped me out of it. I've never been the same since, and I owe a great deal to you.

- I want to stop and take a minute in the busy pace of life to tell you just how much I appreciate the model of _____ (fatherhood, Christian leadership, giving and caring, compassion) you have been to me. In my family, there were no good models of this, and you have been the inspiration that has allowed me to grow in this direction. Thank you.

- As my mentor, you have given so endlessly and tirelessly to me that I would like to take a minute and simply say, "Thank you." If I can ever repay in any way the tremendous debt of gratitude I owe you, just name the place or the person, and I'll be glad to help you or help someone else as you've helped me.

- I just want you to know that the model you were to me as a mentor in my young life is bearing fruit in that I now have _____ protégés. In much the same way that you helped me, I am trying to help them. Your influence continues to influence me and many others through me.

- I know that one of the things you want to do is make a significant difference. I just want to share with you something wonderful that has just happened in my life and to say that without you, it would not have been possible. You have made a major difference in my life!

Adapt these or create your own paragraphs, but please take a minute and drop a note to say thank you to those who have been your mentors over the years.

Take a few minutes right now and recall what each of your early mentors has meant to you and then tell them so in writing.

A TRIBUTE TO MY MENTOR, DR. KENNETH U. GUTSCH
Donald E. Sloat, PhD.
Author and Psychologist

"I'd like you and your wife to come over to my house tonight."

I was blown away by such an unexpected announcement. The flattering invitation came from Dr. Kenneth U. Gutsch, professor at the University of Southern Mississippi, as we were standing outside his office. I was visiting the university several weeks before I was scheduled to enroll as a doctoral student in the counseling department.

With nervous excitement, my wife and I spent the evening at his home. I have a vivid memory of us sitting in his family room. I later learned he "never" invited students to his house and that he was the senior professor in the department.

As my major professor, he made a lasting contribution to my life in two ways. First, he believed in me and supported me. Second, he taught me two significant paradigms that have become second nature to me. The first one was a process to resolve my autonomy issues with my parents. The second was a phenomenological worldview of human perception and behavior that I use every day in dealing with my clients and people I meet.

I cannot imagine how my life would have been without his influence.

Thank you, Dr. Gutsch, for being there and giving to me!

A TRIBUTE TO MY MENTORS
Dr. Norman V. Bridges, President
Bethel College
Mishawaka, Indiana

I am thankful
...to Kenneth Robinson, who taught me to love
     literature,
...to Ray Pannabecker, who taught me how to care
     for the people who work with me and for me,
...to Richard Felix, who taught me how to take risks,
...to my sons, who taught me humility, and
...to my father, who taught me many things,
     including how to live as a committed Christian.

Bottom Line

"Give your friends roses while they are still alive;
don't wait until their funeral."

Robert L. Biehl (my dad)

CHAPTER 15

Honoring Mentors Who Are Already in Heaven

Dr. R.C. Sproul is the chairman of the Ligioner Ministries, a world-renowned theologian, and a best-selling author. On his nationally syndicated radio program, "Renewing Your Mind," he once related an indirect tribute to his mentor, Dr. John Gerstner.

> A few months ago I was preparing to make a trip where I had to speak at a conference. It was scheduled, there were people who had registered for that conference, there was no way I could arbitrarily cancel my presence at that conference.
>
> The night before I was to leave I received a phone call which informed me my beloved mentor, Dr. John Gerstner, collapsed in Pittsburgh while delivering a series of messages. The message I got that night was that he was taken to the hospital in a coma, that he had suffered three strokes, that he was now comatose, and was not expected to live.
>
> And all of a sudden, I was shaken to my roots. Dr. Gerstner is elderly, he has had close encounters with death before, I have anticipated that at some point he will go home, and I often wondered how I would feel if

word came to me that my beloved mentor had died.

I know how I would feel. I would feel as a spiritual orphan. I would feel vulnerable. I would feel alone, I would feel threatened to not have his stabilizing influence in my life anymore just as a son feels when his father is taken from him.

And then finally, through the grace of God, I began to think of what it would mean to him. And I thought, *Wow! If Dr. Gerstner goes home now . . . let's say he goes home this afternoon . . . tonight he'll be sitting at a table talking theology with Luther, and Augustine, and Edwards, and for the first time in his entire life, he'll be having a theological conversation with peers. He's never had that privilege in this world.* And I thought, *Oh, what a glorious thing it will be for him when he crosses the threshold and enters into the heavenly sanctuary.*

The bulletin the next day was radically different. He woke up. The damage was minimal. And two days later he went home. Then a few weeks later he resumed his ministry. And he got the same kind of delay that the apostle Paul experienced in the New Testament. Dr. Gerstner simply has to wait longer to enter into his rest.

There will come a day when your mentor dies. If possible, honor your mentor while he or she is still alive.

A Special Word to Those with Mentors in Heaven

If a mentor who contributed greatly to your life over many years has passed away, I'd like to suggest a project that would be meaningful to you and to many others.

The project is simply this:

First, take a day away by yourself and write down every lesson, every principle, every observation, every rule of thumb, every thought that you can remember your mentor teaching you.

Second, put those thoughts in some kind of nice graphic form. Have them typed or typeset; have them spaced properly; have the grammar checked; get them ready for publication. You can be as simple or as fancy as you care to be in the process.

Third, make a copy of the final version for each of your children and write a cover letter to each of them. Make a copy for the children or grandchildren of your mentor and write a cover letter to each.

This project will take some time and expense, but it will remind you of the role your mentor played. It will be a way of thanking her or him for the input in your life and also of passing that wisdom on to your family as well as the family of your mentor.

The family of your mentor may never have had the access to your mentor that you had as a protégé. Even if they have, they'll appreciate having the tribute as a timeless reminder.

Bottom Line

A written tribute to your mentor can be valuable in helping build your family and your mentor's family over generations.

PART FIVE

A Mentor's Perspective

Just as no protégé has ever started out wanting to fail, no mentor has started a mentor/protégé relationship thinking "How can I let my protégé down? How can I fail miserably in this relationship?" But, how does a mentor become a mentor? What does a mentor look for in a protégé? How does one "do it right"?

The mentor also benefits a great deal from the mentoring relationship. If you involve yourself as a mentor, thirty years from now as you look back on your life, you will find that managing people is where you have gotten your feelings of *success*, and mentoring people is where you have gotten your feelings of *significance* and *satisfaction*.

The following chapters cover a wide variety of subjects which can help you become a mentor with far greater confidence.

CHAPTER 16

What to Look for in a Protégé

Protégés are individuals we see as worthy of the investment of our life energy . . . and whose troubled phone call in the middle of the night is seen as a sign of trust, more than an inconvenience.

Heart Fears about Becoming a Mentor

- What if this person rejects me?
- What do I have to teach someone with all this potential?
- Do I have time for the mentoring relationship?

I've worked with some of the most gifted mentors in the world, but as most mentors begin the process of finding protégés in whom to invest their lives, a wide variety of questions such as these can actually derail the mentoring process before it gets started.

An uneasy feeling or a fearful question may cause you to hesitate in approaching someone as a potential protégé, but do not let that stop you from continuing the process!

One of the ways I have found to be helpful in reducing my uneasiness is a careful wording choice which has made a major difference. It has surprised me how large a difference there is between the somewhat frightening phrase, "I would like to be your mentor" (implication—one and only, solely responsible, exclusive), and the much less threatening phrase "I would like to be *one* of your life mentors" (implication—one of several, partly responsible, nonexclusive). The threat of rejection and miscommunication is far less.

The "Ideal Protégé" Checklist

Once again, I could make a list of hundreds of things to look for in a protégé. It could be broken down to the finest detail. However, what you are looking for is simply a person with less experience than you, in whom you really believe, and whom you want to help reach her or his God given potential over a lifetime. If you have already found this person, you have found your protégé.

The checklist is intended simply to outline additional dimensions of what to look for in a protégé. It can serve as a guide in helping you distinguish between your top three choices of protégé to identify whom you would most like to help over the longest period of time. Before you choose a protégé, does he or she have these qualities?

Your Ideal Protégé Is . . .

1. Easy to Believe in

Your ability to believe in a protégé is very important. You must believe that he or she is a person worthy of the investment of your life energy and believe in his or her future potential.

2. Easy to Like and Spend Time with, Naturally

Regardless of the kind of person you find most attractive as a protégé, look for someone you like naturally and enjoy being with both formally and informally. It is ideal to feel "I want to be with this person," not "I really should (ought to, feel guilty if I don't) call this person." This is a person with whom time seems to fly . . . not drag.

You may respond very positively to people in one age range, or life situation, (for example, kids, teens, young adults), but find it very difficult to relate to people in a different phase (when they get older, married, with children, etc.).

130

It is a reality that some people respond to certain groups better than others. While Galatians 3:28 teaches there are no genders, races, or social positions in the Body of Christ, humanly we do find ourselves more comfortable with certain groups. Much of this can be overcome as we get know others who are different from us, but it is an earthly reality that we tend to be drawn to those most like ourselves.

You may find yourself naturally drawn to troubled children, unwed mothers, or people with special challenges: mental, emotional, physical, or of various other kinds. One of the most important things you can do is simply check with your own heart to explore/define the kind of person for whom God has given you a special warmth, a special care, a special love, or a special compassion. Seek protégés that are consistent with people to whom you are attracted naturally.

3. Easy to Keep Helping

In a mentor-protégé relationship, the mentor is typically more others-centered than the protégé. The protégé often forgets to say, "thank you." He or she may be too caught up in his or her own insecurities and concerns to remember even basic courtesies, like a simple "thank you!" If there is very little emotional reward coming from the protégé, do you care enough about the protégé to continue giving? Here is an example of how to use this checklist to distinguish between protégés. If you had three potential protégés, and if none of the three ever said "thank you," in which one would you naturally find it easiest to continue investing your time and energy?

4. Like Family

You like her or him naturally and want to see her or him do well. Start to see her or him as family. Make a heart commitment to stay deep friends for the long term. *Grab on and hold on* to this young person even when things don't go very well. Choose someone you can imagine yourself still committed to the day you die.

For which of the three protégés you are considering do you have a natural, family type of love? For which one would you be willing to risk, invest, and give with the same kind and level of commitment as you would your own nieces and nephews?

5. Teachable

Is the potential protégé teachable? Is he or she eager to learn? Does he or she seem eager to learn from you? If the protégé is teachable and eager to learn, your natural energy level and interest in helping towards her or his full potential is great. If, on the other hand, he or she seems resistive or unteachable, your interest in continuing to mentor her or him over time will be drastically reduced.

6. One Who Respects/Admires You

Do you sense a natural respect and admiration from the protégé? A natural deference? If so, chances are he or she will be an eager student.

You may spot a protégé that you feel will someday provide leadership for your church, denomination, state, or nation that you could not see yourself providing. Someday, you think this person may go far beyond your own abilities in life. That is okay. Today, however, the person is in a position where, because of developmental phase, nationality, or any number of life situations, he or she looks up to you and is eager to learn from you.

7. Self-Motivated

Will the protégé take the initiative in seeking you out and following through, or will you have to constantly prop your protégé up, cheer her or him on, or get her or him out of a depression? What you are looking for, ideally, is a protégé that is self-motivated, one that will consistently seek you out, take the next step, want to grow, want to learn, want to stretch, and want to reach full maturity.

8. Comfortable With, and To, You

If you find the protégé threatening, chances are he or she is not the right protégé for you. If, on the other hand, you sense that, for some reason, the person finds you extremely threatening to a point where he or she cannot think clearly (distracted) or talk confidently, or if some other form of obvious intimidation manifests itself, you may want to consider a different protégé. You are looking for a person that admires, and respects you, but is not overly intimidated by you.

9. Someone Who Will, or Will Not, Make It Without Me

You may be a person who is not attracted to a young leader with clear "someday" potential to be a future governor, a future president, a future senator, or a future NBA star. You may say, "I'm far more attracted to the one that's not going to make it without someone to care." This is A-Okay!

Sometimes the protégé God lays on a mentor's heart is the person who will not make it if someone doesn't care. Many mentors are far more naturally attracted to the person who may not make it if someone doesn't care for him or her than they are to "super leaders."

Protégé Selection Chart

You may find it easier to do a brief comparison of the three people you have identified as possible protégés before approaching any of them. Hopefully, the simple chart on the following page can help.

Bottom Line

Protégés are individuals we see as worthy of the investment of our life energy and whose troubled phone call in the middle of the night is seen as a sign of trust, more than an inconvenience.

Protégé is...	Protégé One	Protégé Two	Protégé Three
1. Easy to believe in			
2. Easy to like and spend time with, naturally			
3. Easy to keep helping			
4. Like family			
5. Teachable			
6. One who respects/ admires you			
7. Self-motivated			
8. Comfortable with and to you			
9. Someone who will, or will not, make it without you			

CHAPTER 17

Finding and
Approaching a Protégé

I've designed the following checklist to make it easy for you to find and approach a protégé. It gives you a step-by-step guide through the process. You certainly do not need to follow the checklist rigidly, but it may prove helpful by increasing your confidence if you are at all uneasy. As I've said before, whatever you do, don't let your discomfort or uneasiness keep you from taking your first steps. A mentoring relationship is well worth the effort!

Keep this thought in mind throughout your search: your future protégé wants you as a mentor as much as you want her or him as a protégé.

Checklist for Selecting and Approaching a Protégé

❏ 1. Define the essence of what you have to give a protégé.

In approaching a protégé, you may want to identify your single greatest strength, what you do best. Take a minute and think about what strengths you can make available to your protégé. The following list is not intended to be exhaustive; it is simply meant to illustrate the kinds of strengths you may have that are potentially valuable to a protégé. You may have strength in: accounting, bookkeeping, building motorcycles, business, computers, construction, controlling, counseling, decision making, design, discipline, establishing systems, etiquette, evangelism, firing, hiring, horticulture, hospitality, landscaping, mechanics, money management, parenting, preaching, problem solving, risk taking, sales, social skills, teaching, or writing . . . just to name a few.

❏ 2. Review the Ideal Protégé Checklist.

Do this before you begin to think of candidates as well as after you have some people in mind. It will give you a good foundation throughout the process and will increase your ability to make a thoughtful choice.

❏ 3. Make a list of the top three protégé candidates.

Of all the people you know, which three would you most like to mentor over the next few decades? Write their names here:

1. _____

2. _____

3. _____

I recommend that you start with one to three protégés. When your protégés grow to where they are equally capable friends, require less of your time, and are also mentoring, you can begin mentoring others.

❏ 4. Review the definition of mentoring to see which of the three candidates seems to fit best.

Mentoring is a lifelong relationship in which a mentor helps a protégé reach her or his God-given potential.

❏ 5. Ask God to make His will clear.

Ask God to make clear whom He wants to be your protégés. Remember the warning of Psalm 1:1: "Blessed is the man who walks not in the counsel of the ungodly" (NKJV). But also keep in mind that there are no warnings against protégés who are unbelievers.

Note: You may want to have several protégés at a time, helping each win in a different area of life (for example, one spiritual, one professional, and one social).

❏ 6. Meet with the potential protégé.

Once you have selected a potential protégé, in your own time and style approach that person and say something like this:

"I'd like to be one of your life mentors. What I mean by that is simple:
I'd like to put you on my lifelong prayer list.
I'd like to be there when you enjoy success and when you go through hard times.
Every time we meet, I'd like to ask the two mentoring questions:
1. What are your priorities?
2. How can I help?
Bottom line: I'd like to help you realize your full God-given potential over a lifetime. There are a lot of people who would consider a call at 2:00 AM an inconvenience. But before you do something like walk out on your spouse or take your own life, I'm the person you can call. Calling me isn't an inconvenience; it's a command. For the rest of your life, if you get into really deep weeds, you call me!"

❏ 7. Once agreed, review assumptions (see chapter 7).

If the person agrees, be a great mentor! (Chapter 18 will give you five keys.) Start by reviewing the assumptions list so you

137

know what your protégé expects and vice versa.

If the person declines, don't be discouraged. Review your list of potential protégés (you have two other names, right?) and go to step 4 of this checklist. If you need to, start all over with the checklist. You'll eventually find several protégés who need you.

Bottom Line

In seeking a protégé, don't hesitate—initiate!

CHAPTER 18

How to Be a Great Mentor

Before his death in his forties, my uncle Leland Donaldson was truly a great mentor to me. He was my senior by twenty-five years, but once I entered college he started relating to me as a young adult with potential that he wanted to help develop. We would talk for hours at any family reunion, fishing trip, or encounter.

I could tell you of many conversations, but the one which I will never forget was the one at his sickbed which turned out to be his deathbed. Cheryl and I (in our early twenties) went to visit him in the Henry Ford Hospital in Detroit, Michigan, a few days before his death from an inoperable brain tumor. We tried to cheer him a bit, brought the latest bit of family news, and prayed with him.

The very last time we ever talked . . . he was still teaching me! He asked that I read him Philippians 1:21. When I had read the passage he said, "Robert, someday you will realize the meaning of this Scripture like I have. I wish I could live and watch you and your family grow, but it is my time to go and be with the Lord. God could heal me if He chooses. But, I have come to peace with the fact that for me, like Paul, to be with Christ is far better."

As I look back on that bedside scene thirty years ago, I realize Uncle Leland still loved me and was concerned about me and my family. He was trying to encourage me even on his deathbed.

At the risk of oversimplifying, let me suggest that the essence of being a great mentor boils down to five simple things you can do. The rest of this book gives you lots of other important information, but as you begin mentoring, don't lose sight of these five keys.

1. Love

Love your protégé. This alone will take care of a high percentage of the fear in a mentoring relationship because "perfect love casts out fear" (1 John 4:18). It will also help you remain committed to the person because love "endures all things" (1 Cor. 13:7). Love is a key dimension of your role as a mentor. It is important not only to love a protégé but also to express that love with care. Expressions like, "I feel some of what you are feeling. I care that you are hurting. I care that you are struggling right now," can make a lot of difference to your protégé.

Occasionally, say the words "I love you" or write them in a card. Many protégés need to hear the actual words. If you can say them with sincerity, do so.

2. Encourage

As a good mentor, be an encourager, affirmer, recognizer, and cheerleader. Be the person in your protégé's life that keeps giving her or him the message, "You're going to make it!"

It is extremely important for a young protégé to understand that you believe in her or him. Just knowing this can actually be life changing for your protégé. One of the modern tragedies is the number of young people who have no one to believe in and encourage their future potential. When you take your protégé aside and put into words the fact that you see their potential, it substantially accelerates the growth process.

Affirmations from you such as, "You are really smart," "You are really good at that," or "You are going to make it big in this field some day," help heal word wounds from a childhood where your protégé may have been constantly bombarded with unkind and damaging descriptions.

As Claude Robold, a senior pastor, frequently says, "Mentoring helps heal damaged emotions!" This is certainly true in the situation my friend Dr. Allan Beeber experienced. Beeber explains,

> I will never forget when I was emotionally beaten up from some office politics. My mentor was one of the only people who, when he learned of it, sincerely empathized, affirmed my emotions, did not minimize the wrong done, and encouraged me to stay focused on the Lord. I'll never forget his compassion.
>
> I needed a man to enter into the pain with me, and in so doing it accelerated the healing process.

I cannot overemphasize the crucial positive impact your encouragement can have on the life of your protégé. Be on the constant lookout for strengths in your protégé. When you see something he or she does really well, say so. Be prepared to go out of your own comfort zones to express praise, especially when your protégé has tried and succeeded in overcoming some great barrier in life.

For example, I have a somewhat stoic personality. When a protégé asks me to review something, my natural inclination is to offer a simple, flat, stoic, "That's good." What I really mean is, "That's wonderful! You've done an outstanding job! You've surpassed my expectations! This is fantastic! Outstanding! Fabulous! Wonderful! You are to be praised, commended, lauded, and put on a pedestal for this idea! It is a true breakthrough!" But it tends to come out, "That's good."

In the past, a lack of what I would call "effusive communication" has caused protégés to be demotivated in sharing ideas with me. Now I try to force myself out of my comfort zone in order to praise them.

3. Be Open

Share with your protégé. Tell him or her about your failures as well as your successes. Admit, "I'm not perfect either." This is not to give you an excuse to be less than you can be, but to give your protégé a realistic perspective.

4. Check Your Motives

Your job is to build up your protégé. Don't use the protégé for your own purposes. You have agreed to stay on her or his agenda. As a mentor, you are there to help your protégé look good, not to use your protégé to help you look good.

5. Relax

Young people want mentors. Most will be honored and excited that you asked them to be one of your protégés. Be comfortable in the relationship. Love them. Care for them. When you meet, simply ask the two mentoring questions, "What are your priorities?" and "How can I help?" Then relax, and enjoy the relationship.

MY TRIBUTE TO HAROLD EIGINMAN
By David Genn, Executive Director
Awana Clubs International

To Harold Eiginman, I say THANK YOU.

For the hundreds of hours and evenings you spent with me in the Word,

You helped nurture my spiritual roots as they were growing.

For pushing me over the edge to serve the Lord,

You watched me sweat and weep.

For helping me prepare my first message,

Even though I did a terrible job, you gave me a second chance.

For watching me tremble as I presented my ten minutes worth of material in two and a half minutes which seemed like five years,

For not laughing when my first humongous audience turned out to be seventy-five children.

Without your encouragement I wouldn't be where I am today.

Thank you.

Bottom Line

- Protégés are those teachable, eager souls for whom God places in our hearts a lifelong love.
- Protégés need us to love them, challenge them, guide them, affirm them, and introduce them to our closest friends with pride as "one of my lifelong friends!"

CHAPTER 19

Special Instructions to Special Mentors

Aunts and Uncles

Aunts and uncles, you are wonderful people God puts on earth to help nieces and nephews grow up. You're natural mentors. A parent may have a broken relationship with a teenager or young adult, for whatever reason, and you can step in and bring a voice of reason, perspective, balance, and wisdom.

The time to start building relationships with your nieces and nephews that flower into mentoring relationships is when the children are small. Time you spend with your nieces or nephews becoming their friend during the early years sets you up as a voice of credibility in the later years.

Your nieces and nephews need to hear you say, "I love you. I'm here for you. I want to help you if I can. I'm one of the people who really wants to see you do well in life. You've got tremendous ability." You are in a unique position to help your nieces and nephews grow to be healthy, successful adults.

This is especially true when the nieces and nephews have been abused in some way and you can sense that damage has been done. Just take them for a weekend or two, or a week or two, and help them understand that everything is not their fault, they are going to make it, they are lovable, you like them, and they've got a great future ahead of them. Teach them to trust in God.

If you are living several hundred miles from your nieces and nephews, consider sending them a gift every few months. The gifts should not always be clothing or sports equipment. Occasionally, send a gift of education: a book, a tape series (particularly for older children), anything that you think might interest them and might help them get where they are going.

One way or another, it's really important for you to let your nieces and nephews know, "I love you, I'm proud of you, you're going to make it, and I'm here for the rest of my life to help you win if I possibly can."

Couples Who Want to Mentor Other Couples

By looking back on Cheryl's and my maturing years as a couple, I've come to understand that various other couples played a vital role in our development. Many times mature couples invited us into their home for dinner. We watched them act, react, and interact. They modeled how adult couples live life in a way that was different—in some cases worse, in some cases better—than our parents' way. We had to evaluate each couple in light of who we were as people and who our parents were as people. The bottom line is that several couples really made us feel comfortable, cared for, and supported in those early years of married life.

Perhaps you can identify two or three young or less experienced couples you could befriend for two or three years, or ideally, a lifetime. Sit down with your spouse and ask, "Whom would we like to help? Or who won't make it unless a couple like us helps them along?" Then go to those couples and offer to mentor them as a couple.

Minority Leaders

The smaller the group, the more critical the need for leadership. If you have three thousand members and three hundred leaders, you can lose a leader and not be devastated. But if you have one hundred members and only three leaders, losing even one of them is a major trauma.

Any group that considers itself a minority in the society in which it lives desperately needs to understand at a deep level the mentoring process. As a minority leader, identify potential future leaders in your group and give everything you can to mentoring them. The destiny of your group depends on it.

Parents

Parents, until your children are in their high school years, or beyond, you should focus on being parents, not mentors. You may be surprised I feel that way. But consider my reasoning: by definition, a mentor stays on the protégé's agenda. If you're the parent of an elementary school student, you should *not* be on your child's agenda. Rather, your child needs to be on your agenda. You need to be teaching things such as honesty, loyalty, responsibility, discipline, order, and study habits so that your child is prepared to face life.

To go to your young children and say, "What are your priorities?" and "How can I help?" would not be reasonable. On the other hand, when your children get to the point where they have decisions of their own to make and responsibilities of their own in their high school, college, or young married years, you naturally become much more of an advisor. You're still a parent, but you much more closely resemble a mentor.

Certainly by the time your children get married and have children of their own, your role is very similar to that of a mentor. You should basically be asking, "What are your plans?" and "How can I help?"

At this age, your adult child is leaning on you somewhat but is growing progressively stronger to the point where the adult child becomes an adult friend. Today, for instance, Cheryl and I are adult friends of our parents.

Since it doesn't make sense for you to be a mentor to your own children, consider praying for a mentor for them. D. G. Markwell, president and cofounder of Montgomery Christian Educational Radio, Inc., says, "During a transition period in my career, God sent an incredible man into my life. At a time when I was questioning my own abilities, focus, and professional direction, my mentor affirmed my strengths and leadership qualities. As a result of that encounter and others, I began to experience a vitality and a sense of purpose like never before in my work and personal relationships.

"The impact was so significant that I began to think about the positive ramifications this could have on my son. What if he had a mentor who could love him, pray for him, and guide him right from the start? I immediately went to my son's section of my prayer journal and made this entry: *I pray, dear Jesus, for a special man, full of grace and wisdom, to be a mentor to Weston. I pray for him now wherever he is, that you, oh God, will prepare him for this special relationship! Amen!*

"I am excited and thankful that God introduced me to this life changing concept and gave me the opportunity to pass it down to my son at his young age. I can't wait to meet Weston's God-sent mentor!"

Senior Citizens

My father and mother, Bob and Evida Biehl, and my mother- and father-in-law, Joe and Lovina Kimbel, have all served as wise sounding boards for me on many occasions. They are now in their golden years, and I need them today as much as I did twenty years ago.

Retirement years are a time when most people have the time available to be mentors. It may seem like you have little or nothing to offer a protégé. Keep in mind that just being a friend of a young person is often very important. The young person may not have time to just sit and talk, but an encouraging word, a bit of perspective, and a listening ear from you could bear much fruit later on. Remember that young sons-in-law and daughters-in-law are prime candidates for your mentoring perspective, wisdom, and understanding.

I am convinced that people who are eighty years old still need mentors. They need mentors who can help them prepare for ministry, for retirement living, for transition, and possibly for health problems. The point is, we always need mentors. You're never too old to be one or to have one.

A TRIBUTE TO MY MENTOR, JAMES C. ROBERTSON, SR.
By Dr. Joel C. Robertson
President, Robertson Institute, Ltd.

Having met thousands of successful and talented people and having hundreds of friends and several very close relationships, it surprises me that my mentor has been and still is my father. However, it comes as no surprise to anyone who knows him why he has remained in that role for me.

My father has always been a man who is open to change in an ever-changing corporate and personal world. He has always inspired me to determine change based upon progress and biblical principles, not immediate personal comfort.

Whenever I have needed him, he has always given freely, without guilt or expectations in return. My love for him as a son may be natural in a father-son relationship, but my respect for him is due to his consistent and unwavering faith in God, himself, and in his family. His love for God, his family, and me will affect several generations to come.

For these and many other reasons, he has remained my mentor and a solid source of wisdom.

Teachers

I've talked with hundreds of executives over the last twenty years, and I've asked them who has had the most influence at major turning points in their lives. A high percentage of them say it has been a Sunday school teacher, a school teacher, or a professor.

Obviously, as a teacher, you do not have time to mentor every child that comes into your classroom, nor do you have such a natural chemistry that you would want to. But consider the possibility of

149

simply staying with the one or two children per year whom you really like, enjoy, and with you have a natural chemistry. These are kids who seem to be inspired by your personality and look to you for wisdom, reassurance, counsel, and security. You could become one of their mentors for life.

While lecturing on mentoring in Europe, I was approached by a distinguished woman whom I judged to be in her sixties. She came up to me and said, "Bobb, this has been a life-changing message for me." When I asked her how, she said that she had been a fourth-grade teacher in Sweden at the international school and had actually taught the princes and princesses—future kings and queens—of a variety of countries.

She said, "Looking back, if I had simply kept any kind of correspondence with some of these children, today I could influence the thinking of many world leaders. But instead of looking back and saying what might have been, when I go home I'm going to approach each of my grandchildren separately and say to them, 'I am one of the people who will care for you for as long as I live. If I can help you in any way, that is what I want to do.' I want to be a mentor to my grandchildren and help them in any way I can for the rest of my life."

Teachers, you hold a powerful position! You play a critical role in shaping your students' self-confidence, self-concept, and sense of well-being. I encourage you to keep your eyes open for one or two students a year with whom you can stay for a lifetime.

Bottom Line

A few of the relationships, roles, or situations we experience in life (aunts and uncles, mature couples, minority group leaders, parents, senior citizens, teachers) lend themselves exceptionally well to the mentoring process. Take advantage of these special times and relationships to help a few protégés reach their God-given potential life!

PART SIX

Big-Picture Implications

Mentoring is the relational glue that can hold our generation to the last and to the next.

Mentoring is the relational bridge connecting, strengthening, and stabilizing future generations of Christians.

CHAPTER 20

Developing Leaders For the Next Century

I believe that mentoring is the linchpin of Christian leadership development. If the term linchpin is not familiar to you, I'd like to take a minute to explain the concept.

I spent many hours during my junior-high and high-school years on turkey farms belonging to my grandfather and uncles near Mancelona, Michigan. If you've ever driven through Mancelona (on U.S. 131 between Grand Rapids and the Mackinac Bridge), you've seen the Biehl Turkey Farms surrounding this little village.

As a kid working on the farm, I was often the one who was asked to get out of the farm "doodlebug" to hook it up with a trailer. The doodlebug was a 1942 Plymouth with the back end sawed off, which we used to carry feed and pull wagons.

Below you will find a rough diagram of the role a linchpin plays in connecting a trailer to a doodlebug.

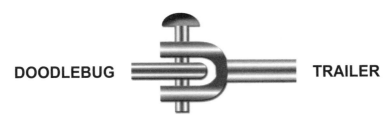

DOODLEBUG   **TRAILER**

Basically, a linchpin is a single piece of steel that is not very large but is very important because with it, the powerful doodlebug (or tractor) can pull a wagon that is hundreds or even thousands of times heavier than the linchpin. Our linchpin cost less than a dollar and weighed less than a pound, belying its importance.

Without the linchpin, the doodlebug could not pull the wagon. I hardly recognized the linchpin as valuable until it wasn't there. If I ever drove off, mistakenly thinking that the linchpin was in place, I could drive for a mile or two before I realized I had left the wagon behind.

> In this simple analogy, the doodlebug is the current generation of Christian leadership. It has a lot of power, but it needs to bring the next generation of leadership (the loaded wagon) along in the process of moving through history.
>
> The linchpin of Christian leadership development is the mentoring process. Our current generation of Christian leadership could easily forget the linchpin and leave the potential of the next generation behind. But through mentoring, we can groom the next generation of leaders, and they can do more than we dared to dream.

Every single organizational unit is a direct reflection of the leadership it's been given, for good or for bad, and it reflects both the leadership's strengths and struggles.

If you took the senior pastor of the largest church in America today and put him in another city, in five years you'd have another major church. If you took a weak pastor and put him at the largest church in the country, in five years you'd have a shell. Every organizational unit is a direct reflection of the leadership it has been given. Leadership is critical to the strength and health of the Christian body.

When I was just starting graduate school I met Bill Bullard for first time. He said, "Bobb, if you want to influence the world, just find a way to influence the top ten people in the world."

What Is Leadership?

Leadership means different things to different people. Since I like to be as clear as possible, let me give you a simple definition from my book *Leading With Confidence*:

> Leadership is knowing what to do next, knowing why that's important, and knowing how to bring to bear the appropriate resources on the need at hand.

Whoever knows these three things will emerge as the leader, whether or not he or she is the positional leader or the elected leader!

Now what is Christian leadership? How does that differ from secular leadership?

> Christian leadership is knowing what God wants to be done next, knowing why He wants it to be done, and knowing how to bring to bear the resources God would bring to bear on the need at hand.

This definition applies to Christian leaders in the pulpit, the cockpit, and the gravel pit. It applies anywhere Christian men and women are serving, in all walks of life.

Where Are All of the Leaders Today?

When you start talking about Christian leadership, one of the first questions that comes up is, "Where are all of our leaders today?" If you want to know where all of our leaders are today, look around you!

I once decided to make a list of my past and present client organizations that are currently developing Christian leaders. I limited my list to groups that were not even in existence in 1950. Here are just a few.

Awana. C. S. Lewis Institute. Campus Crusade for Christ. Core Ministries. Crown Ministries. English Language Institute for China (ELIC). Evangelism Explosion III. Family University. Focus on the Family. Food for the Hungry. Global Missions Fellowship. Heart of a Champion Radio. INJOY. Joy of Jesus. Language Institute For Evangelism (LIFE). Leadership Network. Leighton Ford Ministries. Ligonier Ministries. Minirth Meier/New Life Treatment Centers. Point Man Ministries. Professional Athletes Organization (PAO). Promise Keepers. Serve International. Steve Wingfield Ministries. Woman Today. World Relief. World Vision. Young Life. Youth for Christ.

These organizations are, or are becoming, household words. Most didn't even exist in 1950!

Where are all our leaders? It's my guess that we have maybe five hundred thousand men and women who are in the process of learning to lead in these organizations that did not exist in 1950. Those of you who have as much gray hair as I do remember that in 1950 we had one primary evangelical leader with national visibility, Billy Graham. Today we have a dozen or more! We are making progress in leadership development! No question about it.

You may ask the next obvious and very legitimate question, "If we are developing so many Christian leaders, why are we in such a mess?" The answer is that since 1950 not only has the number of Christian leaders seen a very sharp rise, but so have the number of people and the number of anti-Christian groups. But trust me, we are making great progress.

How Do You Develop Leaders?

I have reflected on this question for the past twenty-five-plus years, and I have reached the following conclusion. Perhaps as much as 80 percent of developing leadership is based on two things:

1. Making sure the leaders you are developing have clear, realistic, measurable priorities (either goals or problems).

2. Being there to help the leaders accomplish their priorities.

This is precisely what the mentoring questions—"What are your priorities?" and "How can I help?"—are all about.

If you are trying to develop a team of leaders, keep it profoundly simple. Help the people on your staff set priorities by asking Steve Douglas's world-class question: "What are the three things we can do (goals we can reach or problems we can solve) in the next ninety days to make a 50 percent difference?" Then help them grow in their ability to reach such priorities. If you do these two things, you will develop leaders.

Perhaps that sounds simplistic to you. I prefer to say it is simple. I admit I was shocked myself when I realized how simple leadership development really is. I've asked many of our top leaders today, "Who mentored you? Who trained you as a leader? Where did you go to be trained as a leader?" They nearly always answer, "No one mentored me, no one trained me, I had no formal education in leadership development." And yet they are leading. How did these men and women learn to lead?

They simply saw a need. They were given, and took, an opportunity. As a result they developed as leaders, one day and one project at a time. In doing so, I believe most of them intuitively followed the two-step development process: they set clear, realistic, measurable priorities and then tried to accomplish them.

Sometimes when I speak on the topic of leadership development, I say to the audience that even though they may think everyone in the room but themselves has had formal classes in leadership, in reality probably less than 1 percent of them have. Then I ask for a show of hands. It is never more than 1 percent.

I really believe that:

- Bible college graduates think to themselves, *I didn't have leadership classes here, but if I had gone to a Christian liberal arts school I would have.*

- Small Christian liberal arts school graduates think to themselves, *I didn't have leadership classes here, but if I had gone to a larger, more prestigious Christian liberal arts school I would have.*

- Larger, more prestigious Christian liberal arts school graduates think to themselves, *I didn't have leadership classes here, but if I had gone to a large state school I would have.*

159

- Large state school graduates think to themselves, *I didn't have leadership classes here, but if I had gone to an Ivy League school I would have.*
- Ivy League school graduates think to themselves, *I didn't have leadership classes here, but if I had gone to a thousand-year-old European university I would have.*
- Thousand-year-old European university graduates think to themselves, *I didn't have leadership classes here, but if I had gone to university in America I would have.*

The point is that, until recently, few schools anywhere in the world taught formal classes in leadership development. Don't feel that you're at a serious disadvantage if you have never had a formal class in leadership development. You are certainly not alone.

This is part of the reason that mentoring is so important to leadership development. A person with a mentor has a major advantage over someone without a mentor. The person with a mentor can go with questions to someone who can help replace trial and error with track record.

Verley Sangster is one of the finest natural leaders I have ever had the privilege of knowing. He has remained a close friend through thick and thin for more than twenty-five years. Listen to the critical role having a mentor has played in his leadership development and in his preparation for the presidency of his organization.

A TRIBUTE TO MY MENTOR
By Verley Sangster, President
Center for Urban Theological Studies (CUTS)
Philadelphia, Pennsylvania

I'll never forget the day I first met the man who was to become my mentor. We were the only two sitting in a steam room at the local YMCA. It was 1968, racial tensions were running strong, and he, a white man, began a conversation with me, a black man. Eventually, our discussion turned to a book, *Think and Grow Rich*, by Napoleon Hill. This young man admitted to me that he

---

wanted to be a millionaire by age thirty-five. Sheepishly, I confessed that I simply wanted to be a millionaire at some point in my life. Our conversation continued; it seemed by chance that we happened to meet every day. Slowly, contrary to the national trends, this white brother and I began to bond.

What cemented our relationship was his offer to be my mentor in the insurance business. Though I did not succeed in that business, what made such an impression was his desire to assist me in my growth and development. He was the first person I ever remember saying to me, "You have potential."

Over the years he continued to be my friend and mentor. At a key point in my career, he said to me, "I want to teach you how to think like a president. Whether you become the president of your organization or not does not matter. The tragedy would be if you were asked, and you were not ready." At that point, he established five ground rules that I have subsequently sought to implement with my protégés:

1. I must remember that I can never thank my mentor enough.
2. I must figure out creative ways to thank him as frequently as possible.
3. I must be clear in my understanding that the mentor-protégé relationship is based upon a natural, personal relationship.
4. We must always communicate honestly, expressing our fears, concerns, doubts, successes, and failures.
5. I must always work hard to apply the principles my mentor teaches me.

I am grateful to God for my friend and mentor. Not only did he mentor me to think like a president, but he prepared me spiritually, emotionally, and intellectually to be the president that I am today.

Entire Movements Come and Go Based on Leadership

I'll never forget when I realized how easy it is to kill the majority of the momentum in an entire movement, such as the civil rights movement or the New Frontier movement. All it takes is a sudden loss of leadership.

On the tragic day Rev. Martin Luther King, Jr., was assassinated, for all intents and purposes, the civil rights movement died. Granted, there are continuing influences from the movement and the country is still making progress here and there, but in my opinion the civil rights movement, as a movement, died that day.

Likewise, the day the assassin's bullets felled President John F. Kennedy, the New Frontier movement, for all intents and purposes, died with him. Granted there are residuals from the movement, but the movement itself died.

During the time of these two assassinations, the following principle became indelibly imprinted on my mind: *Just as you can abruptly stop a movement by assassinating its leader, so you can strengthen a movement by strengthening the leader.* Once I understood that, the importance of strengthening Christian leadership, in any possible way, became crystal clear to me.

That is why I have dedicated my life for many years now to strengthening the great Christian leadership of our generation. Masterplanning Group's purpose statement is, "Strengthening the great Christian leaders and the great ideas of our generation." Mentoring men and women who are leading important movements—strengthening them, protecting them, and encouraging them—is one of the most fundamental and one of the most significant ways we can influence history.

I realize that Christianity is much more than a movement in history. At the same time, I believe it is critical to strengthen the men and women God has raised up to lead the body of Christ in our generation.

Develop Christian Leaders Via the Mentoring Process to Make a Significant Difference

I have been blessed by God to spend many hours one-to-one, behind

162

the scenes after the lights go off, talking about leadership with men and women who are leading our generation—how it develops, how they developed, and the significant influences in their lives. Based on years of interacting with men and women of all ages and nationalities and a variety of theological positions, my personal counsel to you, a Christian leader who wants to make a significant difference, boils down to three short lines:

1. Develop Christian leaders
2. via the mentoring process
3. to make a significant difference

One of my most valued audiocassette tapes is my late Grandfather Gerald Biehl in his last telephone conversation with me. Cancer had put him on his deathbed weighing eighty-five pounds. He was still living near Mancelona, Michigan, and my family and I were living in southern California. In a much weakened, frail, thin voice on that final long distance call, Grandpa urged, "Jim [my middle name is James], teach your kids to love the Lord and go to Sunday school." Later in the week he went home to heaven.

That was the bottom line for Grandpa Biehl. Mine for you is:

Develop Christian leaders . . . via the mentoring process . . .
to make a significant difference.

Bottom Line

Yesterday I asked myself, *If I had five minutes on my deathbed with my adult son and daughter, J. Ira and Kimberly Ann, what would I tell them?*

Develop Christian leaders . . . via the mentoring process . . .
to make a significant difference.

163

CHAPTER 21

A Desperate Need in the Church of the Future

Stop reading for a minute and reflect on this question: "Besides family, who in your church are you absolutely convinced really cares whether you live or die?" Ask yourself, "How many people at my church would still be my friend if I moved away or started attending another church?"

Your answers to these questions tell the real story. Most people I have asked these questions are instantly aware of the need for mentoring relationships within a local church. To be frank, in my opinion that need is *desperate*! Remember, *discipling isn't mentoring*.

Today there are many churches that believe in the mentoring idea and are in the process of introducing mentoring into the life of the church. I applaud them.

At the same time, most churches still assume they are mentoring people if they are discipling them. This faulty assumption results in a church full of well-discipled but relationally disconnected men and women.

Men in the Church

I'd estimate that 5 to 10 percent of the men in a church feel confident evangelizing and feel that evangelism is their life ministry. Some 10 to

15 percent feel confident discipling and feel that discipleship is their life ministry.

My experience with men leads me to believe that 75 to 85 percent feel there is *no significant ministry* for them in the church. These men could and should be challenged, motivated, and mobilized by mentoring. Mentoring provides a vital new ministry option for churches today.

I dream of the day when every child or young person in every evangelical church around the world will have an older man or woman in the church who:

- prays for her or him for a lifetime
- wants to see her or him win
- genuinely cares whether he or she lives or dies

It is my hope that someday each and every child will grow up thinking, *That person really loves me.*

But think for a minute of the number of young people in your church that aren't connected at all to a godly mentor. I'm talking about those who are from eight years to thirty-five years old, the high-school kids coming up, the college kids, the just-marrieds. When students go off to college, do they have a mature person in the church who writes or even calls occasionally? We've got a ways to go in communicating a mentoring-level commitment to the young leaders in our churches.

Pastors

Pastor, I don't expect you to mentor everyone in your church any more than I expect Campus Crusade staffers to mentor every person they lead to the Lord. However, I encourage you to mentor one or two people a year in a specific and special way.

I also suggest looking at the high-school seniors and choosing two a year with whom you have a special, positive chemistry. They may or may not be thinking of going into the ministry. At the very least, have lunch with them during their senior year to help them sort out college and career direction. Put a system in your calendar that reminds you to check in with them periodically over the next two to five years. Call or drop a note saying that you are praying for them during the first few years they are off on their own.

You can be significantly influential with college students in your congregation, as well. Listen to Richard Ensrud, Pastor, Brooklyn Park Evangelical Free Church. "The primary benefit I feel I have received from Bob Salstrom as my mentor is a belief that God wants to use me in a great and powerful way. Growing up, I had no male role model who gave me any sense of destiny for my life. Bob was my pastor while I attended college. He believed in me and believed that God would channel my abilities to further His kingdom. For this I will be forever grateful to my mentor."

According to Claude Robold, pastor of thirty-plus years, "For the pastor who plans to be at a church long term, a major part of pastoring is mentoring laymen."

Consider the major influence Terry Smith, a supportive pastor, had on best-selling novelist Bob Larson (*Dead Air, Abaddon, The Senator's Agenda*).

A TRIBUTE TO MY MENTOR
By Bob Larson

My mentor is Dr. Terry Smith, a Baptist pastor in Dallas, Texas. Though he and I are the same age, he has mentored me because his life experiences as a pastor have been different from mine as a writer and broadcaster. He has given me balance by helping to guide my decisions with scriptural criteria, and he has unselfishly invested himself in our friendship.

During a most difficult time in my life, he called me on the phone every single day for several years to monitor my emotional and spiritual health.

Though my media ministry reaches a much larger audience than his pastorate, he has taught me that the measure of one's value in the Kingdom of God is not based on quantity.

Every time I broadcast, Terry's voice speaks through

> my voice. When I write a book, his hours of spiritual
> encouragement flow through my pen. My ministry has
> become his ministry. Every man needs a friend and
> mentor like Dr. Smith. And everyone in the Lord's work
> needs someone like this to remain faithful with God.

Pastors, over your lifetime select about twelve people who come through your church whom you will follow, support, and strengthen over their lifetime.

I also urge you and every other pastor in the world to consider playing the role of mentor in the lives of younger pastors. Consider the influence Dr. W. A. Criswell had on Dr. Robert Jeffress, pastor of First Baptist Church of Wichita Falls, Texas.

A TRIBUTE TO MY MENTOR
By Dr. Robert Jefferies

For thirty years I had the opportunity to sit under the ministry of Dr. W. A. Criswell. Seven of those years were spent serving on his staff at the historic First Baptist Church of Dallas. No man has made a greater impact on my life and ministry than Dr. Criswell.

On a personal level, he has been a part of every significant event in my life. When I was five years old, he knelt down with me in his office and led me to faith in Christ. When I was seven, he baptized me. He counseled with me at age fifteen when I felt called to the ministry. Later, he officiated at our wedding ceremony. He presided over my ordination service while I was a seminary student and conducted the memorial service for my parents. I will be eternally grateful to him for his faithfulness as a pastor to me and my family.

But Dr. Criswell's influence in my life goes beyond

that of a loving pastor. He has also modeled for me what it means to be a preacher of God's Word. To put it simply, everything I have learned about being a pastor I have learned from Dr. Criswell. I will always be grateful to Dr. Criswell for taking a chance and hiring me as his associate when I was fresh out of college. I will never forget his words to me in our interview: "Son, remember, you don't have to answer to anyone in the church but me. And all I will ever do is pray for you."

Dr. Criswell has often asked the rhetorical question, "Why is it that we are not judged by God the moment we die? The reason is that a man's influence does not cease when he dies. It continues for years and years beyond his death." I am convinced that Dr. Criswell's influence upon Christendom will be felt for generations to come because he has devoted his life to instilling God's Word in the hearts of people.

Women in the Church

Mature women of the church . . . you are desperately needed by young women today. The women of Coast Hills Community Church in Aliso Viejo, California, had a fall women's retreat. They had speakers. They had special events. They had special food. It was a successful, well-attended retreat. One of the optional program offerings was a session that the planning committee did not know if anyone would attend. It was called "Women of Wisdom."

Now to properly understand the planning committee's uncertainty, you need to know that Coast Hills was a very young church, filled with young executive couples in their mid-twenties to mid-thirties. White-haired women were not in the majority. This session was led by some of the elders' wives and other mature women in the church. No one knew if the young women at the retreat would choose to spend the delightful sunny California afternoon outside or at a meeting with "older women."

As you probably guessed, it was the best-attended session of the entire retreat. It was supposed to last an hour, and it went for two-and-a-half hours. Two-and-a-half hours of sincere questions from the young women of the church and pure, open answers from the mature women of the church.

I'm sure you have read Titus 2:3-5 many times in your life. Reviewing it at this moment might be refreshing and enlightening.

> Likewise, teach the older women to be reverent in the way they live, not to be slanderers or addicted to much wine, but to teach what is good. Then they can train the younger women to love their husbands and children, to be self-controlled and pure, to be busy at home, to be kind, and to be subject to their husbands, so that no one will malign the word of God (NIV).

WOMEN MENTORING WOMEN
Ways to Start, Maintain, and Expand a Biblical Women's Ministry
By Vickie Kraft

Women are longing for friendships with other women. James Dobson reminds us that the loneliness and isolation women feel today is not because men have changed in the last century. It is because there has been a breakdown in the communication between women and women. With the increased mobility people have and the breakdown of the extended family, women's opportunities for relationships have been greatly curtailed.

In previous generations women did things together—cooked, sewed, quilted, canned, raised children, and mostly talked! We have largely lost that sense of community and today the church must step in and help women get to know and love each other, filling the gap left by the disappearing extended family. Serving on committees and boards together, taking an elective together, going on retreats, praying together—all provide opportunities for friendships to develop. Fellowship is more than coffee and cake; it is working together toward a common goal.

There has also been an enormous growth in the number of singles living alone. In the 1950s only 6 percent of the population lived alone as compared to approximately 24 percent today. That figure includes, of course, those who have never married, the widowed, and the divorced. Single parent families are increasing every year. No one can even measure the damage that divorce is having on the children—and these children are the parents of our next generation.

How can we minister to singles? This is an increasing concern of the local church. One-third of my home church is single; therefore, we have a minister to singles and a strong singles' ministry. I recognize that most smaller churches do not. However, even with our active singles' ministry, we have found that single women still desire to be connected to women of the church. They get tired of being with just their peers. There is a lack of reality in a life where there is no connection to the generations before you or after you. Single women also have many questions, questions that need the counsel of older, spiritually mature women.

Women want female mentors to teach them to be wives and mothers. Additionally, young professional women need and want mentors just as much as, if not more than, young professional men do. Unfortunately, young women have fewer professional mentors from whom they can choose. There is a great need for professional women who'll be mentors. Young women typically ask, "To whom do I go? My aunts and my mother never worked outside the home. They were not professional women. I don't have a good model of how to be a competent, mature, Christian woman in a professional setting."

We need the mature women in the Christian community today mentoring the next generation of women.

Youth Workers

Youth workers, your job is extremely important! You have many kids come through your program each year. You could identify one or two who have exceptional potential or with whom God has bound your heart. Be proactive in their future! Call them at college, in the military, or on their new job.

Make a list of people you want to call once a quarter. Say, "How are you doing? How's school? What have been your biggest adjustments to being away? Is there any way I can help you? I'm praying for you. I believe in you. You're going to make it!" Help them sort our their priorities. A lot of times young people on their own for the first time get disoriented and discouraged because they don't have clear priorities in front of them.

You have hundreds of hours of relationship invested in some of these kids, but just three hours a year for the next thirty years could maximize all of those hours you've invested in some of the brightest people who have come through your youth program. You're in a unique position to be able to minister effectively long-term with some of these kids, and I encourage you to take full advantage of it.

David Horner, senior pastor of the Providence Baptist Church, is an example of the rewards of investing in eager young people. After spending many days consulting with David and his entire leadership team, I can say with complete confidence that David is one of the finest young pastors and leaders in America today. The church he planted a few years ago is a solid, growing church with thousands in regular attendance. But once David was "just a kid in the youth department."

A TRIBUTE TO MY MENTOR, J. L. WILLIAMS

By David Horner, Senior Pastor
Providence Baptist Church, Raleigh, North Carolina

More than twenty-five years have passed since I first met J. L. Williams. At the time, he was working with high school students through a local YMCA. He had a contagious excitement about Christ that made me want what he had, a living relationship with the Lord. Along with scores of other students, I became involved in studying the Scriptures with him in weekly Bible studies and was soon learning what it meant to grow in Christ.

I caught a vision of a living faith in J. L., which has led me to pursue him for advice and direction all through the years. The passion I have today for teaching and preaching God's Word began as I listened to him and started a lifetime process of learning how to make the Scriptures clear. I learned from him that the eternal truths that have so changed my life can come alive for others. I will long remember how humbled I was when he and his family came to visit our church one Sunday morning when I was preaching. After years of listening to him, there he was listening to the message the Lord had given me! What an encouragement he has been by supporting my ministry all these years.

One of the great joys my wife, Cathy, and I have is the close friendship we have with J. L. and his wife, Patt. In the past several years, we have shared family milestones together, ministered together in church conferences and seminars, and traveled together overseas on various mission trips. I learn from him each time I am with him and never tire of his company, his insights, his vision, his boundless energy, and his constant encouragement to me to press on for the glory of Christ. Although he would probably never define our relationship that way, J. L. is my mentor. His impact on my life has been significant because he cared enough to invest himself in helping me become a godly leader in my family and in the body of believers I serve as pastor. To paraphrase the apostle Paul, "I thank my God upon every remembrance of him."

Introducing Mentoring to Your Church

Take Thirty Seconds to Imagine . . .
What would happen if the mature men and women of your church decided to hide the children and young people of your church in their hearts for a lifetime?
What if each child had a lifelong prayer supporter, a lifelong cheerleader, a lifelong partner to call before walking out on a marriage or jumping out of a window after a devastating financial loss?
What difference would it make?

What difference would it make if every one of your sons and daughters had an adult in the church, a surrogate uncle or aunt, who would support and protect your child for a lifetime in a healthy mentoring relationship? By now I hope even the early skeptics would agree that it would make all the difference in the world!

Could this idea be the new challenge you have been asking God to give you? The new path you have been asking him to make clear? What difference would your leadership in mentoring in the church make over the next fifty to one hundred years? Are you willing to share your vision with your church?

In many churches, we've said we'll let mentoring relationships develop naturally. But what if they don't develop naturally?

How can you make sure every willing person in your church is vitally connected for a lifetime to a mature, experienced, loving person who cares if he or she lives or dies?

Establishing a Church-Based Mentoring Program

In all honesty, mentoring in the church is a relatively new, typically experimental idea. I am aware of few programs that have been long established and successful. As you begin thinking through your church mentoring program, there are some guidelines to follow. If I seem to write strongly about certain points, I intend to. Some aspects are make-or-break for a mentoring program. And because mentoring is so powerful, significant change can be made if certain guidelines are honored.

Confidentiality Is Critical

To develop a healthy mentoring program, you *must* protect confidentiality. This is especially true in a small group setting where "prayer requests" on behalf of your protégé can sometimes become little more than gossip. The rule of thumb for confidentiality is that anything that the protégé has not said in public is assumed to be confidential until that person says it's okay to share it. In other words, in the mentoring relationship, it's critical to assume confidentiality of everything the protégé says until the protégé gives you specific permission not to be confidential in a given area.

Lifelong Ministry

For some individuals, mentoring is their ministry just as calling in hospitals or teaching a fourth-grade class is someone else's ministry. Mentoring is, in fact, a ministry that offers a supportive, nurturing, encouraging person a lifetime of satisfying service. And unless otherwise agreed upon, mentors in your program should approach each mentoring relationship as a lifelong commitment.

Not 100 Percent Successful

You can try as hard as you want, and the mentors and the protégés can try as hard as they want, but there will be misfires. There will be mentors and protégés who think they'll get along, think they are very compatible, think there would be great benefit in a relationship like this over time, only to see the relationship fall apart. Don't let that

175

discourage you. Simply analyze the situation carefully to see where the problem came from, and help both individuals find another mentor or protégé in the church.

A One-to-One Ministry, Not a Group Activity

Mentoring typically doesn't happen on a group-to-one basis. It's a one-to-one ministry, and participants need to understand that and be comfortable with it. You can have a men's group or women's group that meets to discuss benefits, direction, inspiration, and information about mentoring. You can even conduct how-to training and problem-solving, so that it is a "mentoring group." Always remember that it is simply a group that discusses and facilitates mentoring. Ninety-nine percent of mentoring happens one-to-one.

A Process, Not an Event

Mentoring takes time. With some young people it takes many years to get to the point where you feel they have stabilized, matured, and become ready to be on their own. It is not a one-time emphasis event with a lot of hurrahs, cheering, and excitement that are forgotten the next day. It is a process, a ministry of the faithful people of the church who enjoy relationships that last over time.

A Quiet Movement, Not a Flashy Program

Mentoring is probably not a program that will appear on your church billboard. Your letterhead may never say, "Mentoring program available." It is not a fad program to start one year and drop the next. It is a movement for quiet people who enjoy working behind the scenes, for no pay or glory, helping other people win.

Eight Steps for Launching a Mentoring Program at Your Church

Please understand that these steps represent flexible, fluid concepts. You can rearrange, adapt, add to, skip—whatever is needed to get your program started. This is simply a brief outline of one track on which you can run.

1. Brief Your Pastor and the Board First

Before you introduce the concept of mentoring to the church, introduce it to your pastor and the board. Many pastors see their role as one of mentoring many in the congregation. If your pastor is not familiar with the mentoring concept, help him see the benefits to the church. Mentoring can provide more intimate relationships, stability for people under pressure, the attractiveness of friends coming to church to see other friends, and the possibility of the pastor's counseling load being lightened.

2. Appoint a Champion

A champion is a leader, a spokesperson, a driving force, a sparkplug, a person who brings the program along and who keeps the mentoring concept always in the mind of the congregation. Your mentoring program should have a champion who, in appropriate ways, optimizes opportunities to promote mentoring. The champion tells inspiring stories of mentoring, makes resources on mentoring available, and does whatever else is necessary to keep the mentoring flame burning.

3. Establish a Steering Committee of People Interested in Mentoring

4. Develop a List of Members Who Would Like to Have a Mentor or Become One

Whenever a person on the list finds a mentor or becomes one, check off her/his name.

Name of each person on the mentoring team	Has a mentor	Has a protégé
Sally	✓	✓
Sam	✓	✓
Carl		✓
Carole	✓	

The mentoring program is not high-maintenance. You don't have to check on people to see if they are or are not doing something. What you do is set the relationships in motion and then let the natural momentum of the relationships pull the program along. Highlighting the mentoring idea whenever possible will keep it alive, as will an occasional newsletter and opportunities to attend mentoring conferences from time to time.

5. Have an Intergenerational Retreat

One of the main problems in our churches today is that we have few activities which involve all ages of men and women. Children have their program, teens have their program, and seniors have their program. Where are the opportunities for a more mature person with a lot of experience to meet a less-experienced person so the natural chemistry can start? Consider having a church retreat for all men and boys, and then another one for all women and girls, where all of the activities are designed to give potential mentors opportunities to discover natural chemistry with potential protégés.

6. Introduce Mentoring to Special Groups in the Church
    A. Show a video–*Mentoring: How to Find a Mentor and How to Become One* (See Appendix D)
        Show a video about mentoring to a small group. Excitement is often sparked because members see that others are interested.

    B. Give each person a mentoring booklet
        Distribute the booklet *Mentoring: How to Find a Mentor and*

How to Become One (See Appendix D) to everyone in the special group (or at least make sure they know about the booklet). If you think twenty people will show up, order twenty booklets. That way, after they see the video, they can go home, do some reading, and ask a mentor or protégé to consider a mentoring relationship.

C. Suggest that those who are really interested in mentoring read this book—pass your copy around.

D. Read some of the tributes in this book to spice up the meeting with inspiration.

Also, a lot of churches have an occasional "moment for missions;" maybe you could introduce a "moment for mentoring." You could read a tribute from this book or have someone from the church give a live personal tribute to her/his mentor.

7. Have a Mentor-Protégé Retreat

In a retreat setting mentors and protégés simply spend time together, talk together, plan together, pray together, and generally get to know each other in a much deeper way. Have the mentors invite their protégés to this retreat and line up speakers who understand that the audience is made up of mentors and protégés.

8. Train and Encourage Mentors

Lack of confidence is the single greatest concern on the part of mentors as well as protégés—confidence that I'll be accepted, confidence that I'll know what to do, confidence that I'll have something significant to say, confidence in general.

One option is to have a support group for mentors where mentors meet once a month to discuss the mentoring process, to ask questions, and to get answers. You may want to read something from this book or watch a video. Do anything that will rekindle the group's excitement about the mentoring process.

Ask yourself in your heart of hearts, where no one else sees, if you are confident that all of the young people in your church—the kids, the teens, the young leaders, the young families—have someone who cares whether they live or die. Never lose the dream of building a mentoring network where all of the young people have lifelong mentors who care for them, want to see them do well, and will be there for them for the rest of their life. Keep that dream alive.

Bottom Line

Imagine the difference it would make if in each church one person would become a mentoring champion and help people really understand what mentoring is.

Then imagine the difference it would make if all of the young people in your church had mature believers to hide them in their hearts for a lifetime, to be lifelong prayer supporters and lifelong cheerleaders, lifelong partners to call when there seemed to be no one else to call.

This Is The Mentoring Dream!

PART SEVEN

The Future of Mentoring

Do you have a dream in your heart? Have you been seeking one? Frequently, I try to help protégés, friends, and clients define their dream by asking the following question:

"How can I make the most difference for God in my lifetime?"

If you will tell me your answer to this question, I will tell you your dream.

CHAPTER 22

Consider Making Mentoring Your "Personal Dream"

In your heart of hearts, where no one has ever seen, ask yourself these two questions:

1. Does what Bobb has been saying about mentoring make sense to me?
2. Is it possible that mentoring should become my personal dream?

As I alerted you early in the book, to me this is not just another book. I'm here to help you see the rightness of finding and becoming a mentor, of developing a few relationships of influence that will last a lifetime.

INFLUENCE

When you influence a child, you influence a life.

When you influence a parent, you influence a family.

When you influence a president, you influence a corporation.

When you influence a pastor, you influence a church.

When you influence a leader, you influence all who look to him or her for leadership.

To influence anything is to have an effect on it, to change its course, or to make a difference—no matter how small—in the outcome. Dr. Bob Pierce, the founder of World Vision, used to say, "Just because you can't do everything doesn't mean you can't do something."

You may say, "I agree with you, Bobb. When I was a kid, I had a feeling of destiny. When I was a kid I felt like someday I was going to do something great. But right now I work at a place where I don't feel much destiny. I feel like I'm not sure if I'm making any difference. Bottom line: I feel stuck, put on the shelf, lost in a sea of mediocrity, bound up, underpowered, and without hope of making a significant difference in this world."

You Can Start Mentoring Tomorrow

Mentoring is something you can do to make a major difference no matter where you live or what work you do. Today it may feel like it is impossible for you to influence the world. You feel stuck with limitations like living in a small town, attending a small church, having little education, or working a menial job. In other words, you may feel like Lee Donaldson.

Lee Donaldson was my maternal grandfather. He loved me. He grabbed on to his young grandson and hung on. He confronted me when I did wrong. He taught me to do right. Grandpa had a second-grade education and lived in a town of about eight hundred people. He was a shoe repair man. He was the janitor at the church. He did odd jobs. He probably never made more than three thousand dollars a year. He had no idea that someday his curly-headed grandson would write twenty-plus books and that you would be reading it. But he made a significant difference in my life and, I hope, in yours!

You May be Mentoring an Abraham Lincoln

Stop reading for a minute and think about this: As you mentor one child, one young person, or one young adult, you may be influencing the next Jim or Shirley Dobson, David or Shelby Genn, Billy or Ruth Graham, Josh or Dottie McDowell, or Adrian or Joyce Rogers. In that sense, you never really know who your protégé is or what your influence will be as his or her influence trickles through history.

The future governor of your state or a future president of our country might be in your elementary-school classroom today or in your Sunday school classroom on Sunday. He or she may be the irritating kid down the street. You never know what part your influencing, strengthening, and mentoring one child will play in shaping history.

I've heard a lot of teachers say things like, "In my classroom, I'd rather have what Dr. James Dobson calls a strong-willed child I could help shape into a leader for the future than a compliant child who doesn't have the character strength to be a leader." Sometimes the child that is the most disruptive, or the teenager that is the most difficult to control, is the one with the most leadership potential—if it can be channeled in the right direction for God.

I will never forget a discussion I had with Steve Wingfield. Steve is a lifelong friend who is a crusade evangelist. Steve once attended one of our Advanced Leadership Retreats, where he told the story of how his fourth-grade teacher once came up behind him, put her hand on his shoulder, gently squeezed his neck just enough to get his undivided attention, and said, "Steve, someday when you grow up, that great voice of yours is going to be used to tell people about God, but for right now you need to be quiet." That is a great example of a teacher encouraging a child's strength and at the same time establishing clear limits.

Consider the child that is the most difficult to deal with, the rambunctious teenager, the young adult leader who has the greatest potential for disruption, and ask yourself, "What might this person become someday if he or she gets enough love and mentoring today?" Try to imagine what this child or young person will be like at fifty or sixty years of age with and without mentoring.

One of the most inspiring mentoring stories I have read is the historic account of the man who was Abraham Lincoln's mentor.

It was in 1800, a century and a half ago, that Mentor Graham was born to Jeremiah Graham and his wife, Mary, up in the northwest corner of Green County, Kentucky. By the time he was seven he was the star pupil in Schoolmaster Borun's school and while other boys were "fighting Indians" in their play Mentor was going through the few books available in a frontier community.

Nine years later, south of Hodgenville, in LaRue County, less than fifteen miles distant, Abraham Lincoln, a figure known to the whole world and revered by that world, perhaps as no other person, was born in like lowly circumstances.

Mentor Graham had an uncle Robert, a doctor, who had books and great learning, for that day and age, and to Doctor Robert's house he went to live when about ten years of age. He rode behind the good doctor as he made his horseback rounds and school for Mentor was a continuous affair in the home and on the horse. He learned much that the ordinary youth of the 1800s would never know through these contacts for two years.

Then he was sent to the Brush Creek Academy, and, at sixteen, taught the Brush Creek school. It was then he married Sarah Rafferty, not yet fourteen years old.

He was a frugal as well as a bookish young man and by surveying, carpentry, farming, and his school earnings he acquired considerable property. Later he taught the town school in Greenburg, the county seat. Illinois was then a young state and many of his kinfolk had moved up into Sangamon County near New Salem and after a trip up to see the country Mentor Graham decided to go to Illinois and in October 1826 he and Sarah and the child Almira made the journey up to New Salem. Graham made his home just west and north of town on Green's Rocky Branch of the Sangamon River.

In the meanwhile Abraham Lincoln, Mentor's junior by nine years, was learning his three "R's" and at eight, his family, always poor, had moved to Gentryville, Indiana. Lincoln, like Graham, loved books, but he had few opportunities to read them.

In 1828 he made a trip down the Ohio and Mississippi to New Orleans and after witnessing the slave markets there, acquired a hatred of slavery. In 1829 Lincoln first came to New Salem. This time as a flatboatman on the

Sangamon. His flatboat "hung up" on the Rutledge-Cameron dam and it was then that Lincoln and Graham first came together.

Graham with his four years in the new area had become a fixture and, with his usual industry and thrift, had acquired a competence. Lincoln was then, according to himself, still "driftwood."

Graham was an uncompromising foe of liquor and slavery and, in the backwoods community, where the roughs of the frontier gathered, was respected, but not liked, by the great part of the community.

In 1831 Lincoln and Graham came together in an official capacity. In August of that year there was an election and people of learning, capable of conducting such an event, were few and far between. Lincoln, despite his protestations of incompetence, was drafted as a clerk of the election.

Something was holding the drifter in New Salem and it soon developed that the something was Ann Rutledge, the beautiful Titian haired daughter of miller and tavern keeper. She was studying with Mentor Graham for entrance into the Academy. Lincoln was also studying in February 1833 and for six months thereafter Lincoln lived at the home of Mentor Graham. There the two young people met and studied together. In July of that year the engagement of Lincoln and Ann Rutledge became known. The romance of this great man's life thus was under the roof of Mentor Graham.

Lincoln at one time wanted to give up further study, but it was Mentor Graham who argued that a man, if he was to pursue public life, must have a perfect knowledge of grammar and he told Lincoln where he could obtain a Kirkland's grammar.

Thereafter Lincoln studied grammar under the tutelage of Mentor Graham. He recited his lessons in a fence corner or other place where the pupil and master might meet. Graham as a teacher was famous for his emphasis on

189

correct word usage, succinctness of speech and of writing and it cannot be doubted that the effective and terse style of Lincoln, best exemplified by his Gettysburg address, found its inception in the teachings of Mentor Graham.

Graham as a surveyor taught the art to Lincoln. While at New Salem, Lincoln was in turn a mill hand, clerk, postmaster, and finally in 1834 in the Illinois legislature after being defeated in his first try of political favor. Two years later Lincoln was admitted to the bar of the State of Illinois. It was in the hard times of 1845 that Lincoln as a lawyer, sued Graham, for a debt of one hundred dollars that he owed and then Lincoln-like, showed him how he could raise the money to pay the debt.

Mentor Graham was never a man to be idle and between terms of teaching he peddled books, did farming and surveying, and always took a great interest in all public affairs.

When Lincoln was nominated for the Presidency, his neighbors in New Salem, and particularly Sarah, could not believe ears. When the time came for his inauguration, Mentor Graham had to go and, despite the cost, go he did. As he was growing somewhat deaf at sixty-one, he sat himself down, well in front that he might hear well. Lincoln spied him out and sent for him to sit on the platform with him. This was indeed the happiest day of Mentor's life. Perhaps the saddest was when the news of Lincoln's death came to him.

The week he died the *Blunt Advocate* was established as a daily paper and in Volume I, No. 1, dated October 7th, 1885, the obituary of Mentor Graham appeared on the front page. It read as follows:

AN AGED PERSON GONE

Mentor Graham died at the residence of his son H. L. Graham, in this place on Sunday evening (Oct. 4) last. Mr. Graham was born in Hardin County, Kentucky, in 1802 moved to Illinois. At 17 years of age he engaged in teaching and continued in that profession for 55 years.

Abraham Lincoln and Governor Yates were among his pupils.

Those who, like the writer, first knew Mr. Graham when the weight of years had destroyed the vigor of manhood, can appreciate the worth of his character and but faintly conceive the influence he exerted in molding the minds of men who bore so large a part in guiding and preserving our nation during the period of the Rebellion.[1]

Mentoring one to twelve protégés over your lifetime may be your destiny. It may be the way you change history. It may be the way you make a major difference. It may be the reason you are on this earth today, to mentor even one person who wouldn't make it without you. Fifty years from now people may look back at you as we would look today at Mentor Graham—totally unknown to the watching world, but front row center in your protégé's special guests list.

The Snowball Analogy

The following is one of my favorite word pictures, showing the leadership leverage in the mentoring concept.

When I was sixteen years old, I walked out of the house one day, and my eyes froze on the thermometer. It was literally forty-seven degrees below zero, and there was no wind chill factor! My point? Being from northern Michigan I know cold and snow!

Now you've packed snowballs, right? You know the difference between powder-snow weather, where you can't pack, and packing-snow weather, one of those warm early spring days when you can really pack a snowball. You know the difference, right?

Imagine with me for a minute that we climb into a mountain-skiing Bell helicopter, and are flown to the top of a mountain. This mountain is unusual in that the top is a perfectly round circle with a twenty-foot diameter and is as flat as a billiard table. When we look off the edge of the flat top, all we see in every direction are beautiful slopes all the way to the bottom, exactly twenty miles in all directions.

It has been snowing for three weeks, but for the last day or two it has been unseasonably warm. Today there is a crystal-blue sky and diamond-white snow, and it is absolutely perfect packing weather.

We go over to the edge and look down twenty miles to the bottom. There's not a tree on the hill. We think, *What if we want to make a significant difference in the amount of snow that is on this mountain? What if we took a little snowball, rolled it up into the size of a snowman's head, and gently pushed it over the side?*

What would happen? On this imaginary mountain the pitch of the hill is perfect for keeping a snowball rolling, so we make a snowball and start it down the hill. The snowball starts to roll, and roll, and roll, gaining momentum clear to the bottom of the mountain.

Now, just imagine for half a second how big that snowball will be twenty miles later! If it holds together, it will be three hundred stories tall, bigger than the size of the world's largest football stadium!

Now imagine for a minute that you can roll as many snowballs off as you want. Some may get stalled just a short way down the hill as they hit a stump or a rock hidden under the snow. But twelve of them will go all the way to the bottom. And will they be huge!

That's what mentoring is in my mind!

Every time you take on a protégé, it's like picking up a handful of snow. You pick her or him out in life, and you say, "Let me pack you up, start you down through life, and if you have any questions, if you get stuck up down there, let me know, and I'll just come down and give you a little shove, and you can roll on down the hill." Twenty miles, or twenty years, later, imagine the impact and influence on history!

Each One Mentor One

Consider one other profoundly simple example of how mentoring can work. Dr. Frank Laubach's epitaph ascribes to him the following title: "The man who taught the world to read."

Dr. Laubach popularized the phrase "each one teach one." Via his simple four-word strategy of teaching one person to read under the condition that each would teach another to read, several million people have now experienced the thrill and freedom of reading for the first time. The chain continues to this day, long after his death. Today the Laubach Method has more than eighty thousand volunteers worldwide.

> Pause for sixty seconds and try to imagine the implications of this:
> You mentor 12, who mentor 12, equals 144!
> who mentor 12, equals 1,728!
> who mentor 12, equals 20,736!
> who mentor 12, equals 248,832!
> who mentor 12, equals 2,985,984!

Is an unbroken chain of mentors realistic? Probably not! But the point is clear. If only a small fraction of protégés follow through by mentoring someone else, a significant difference will be made in the number of leaders over the next few centuries—or until the Lord returns!

I first met Dr. Robert Coleman (we called him "Clem" at that point) when he was a youth speaker at the Brown City, Michigan, Missionary Church camp. I was sixteen years old. His book *The Master Plan of Evangelism* has been reprinted dozens of times and has likely sold millions by this point. Listen to the words of one of his protégés, my friend Steve Wingfield. Imagine the chain of influence in history started by a man like Dr. Coleman, and then realize that you can start just such a chain!

A TRIBUTE TO DR. ROBERT COLEMAN
By Steve Wingfield, President and Evangelist
Steve Wingfield Ministries, Inc.

I will always remember the day Dr. Robert Coleman offered me the opportunity to become one of his boys. Years before, I read his book *The Master Plan of Evangelism* and used it as a model in my life and ministry.

I will be eternally grateful for the time, prayer, encouragement, motivation, and example this godly man has invested in my life and ministry. I am not only a better man because of this relationship, but also keenly aware of the responsibility that is mine to serve others as a mentor. The desire of my heart is to be faithful to Christ by passing on the blessing to as many people as possible. "And the things you have heard me say in the presence of many witnesses entrust to reliable men who will also be qualified to teach others." (2 Tim. 2:2 NIV).

Our primary calling as believers is to pass on the blessing. We do that by investing ourselves in other people. I am who I am today because of the grace of God and the blessing that other people have passed on to me. I thank God that my mentors, Dr. Robert Coleman and others, saw in me not just who I was, but who I could be in Christ.

Mentors are Like Faithful Clydesdales

Race horses are lightning fast for the short run, but they run out of steam for the long run. Clydesdales won't win any races, but they are strong for the long haul. You may not see yourself as a super-fast, showy person. That is great! Keep mentoring day after day, week after week, year after year for the rest of your life. Be strong for the long haul.

Lloyd Murray, a lifelong friend, told me one day that one of his early mentors told him as a kid, "Lloyd, If you will read one complete book on building bridges, you will know more than 97 percent of the nation's population about the topic of building bridges."

Well, you now know more about mentoring than 97 percent of the people in the world—what it is, why it is important, and how it works.

Consider taking a ten-to-eighty-year view of mentoring (depending on your age, of course). Plan to stay with it for the rest of your life, as I plan to stay with it for the rest of my life! Consider being part of a group of faithful people who are committed to mentoring as a personal dream.

If you have had a mentor . . .

What difference has it actually made in who and where you are today?

Do unto others what someone else has done for you.

If you have not had a mentor . . .

What do you wish, in your heart of hearts, a mentor would do for you? Do unto others as you would have them do unto you!

My prayer for you as you read this book is two-fold.

First, take a moment and thank your mentors for the investment they have made in your life.

Second, determine to pass on the blessing by being a mentor.

Bottom Line

- It is time to act!
- Please join me on the mountain of life for the rest of your life.
- Be a lifelong protégé and a lifelong mentor.
- Develop lifelong relationships, in which you grow into your God-given potential and help your protégés grow into their God-given potential.
- Only in heaven will we even begin to grasp the results!

[1]This account is from a simple brochure by R. Bryant Mitchell entitled "MENTOR GRAHAM."

PART EIGHT

Mentoring Information:

ADDITIONAL RESOURCES TO MAXIMIZE YOUR MENTORING ABILITY

Bibliography of Mentoring Resources

Special thanks to Stephen E. Olsen and Dr. Skip Lewis for their contribution to this bibliography. The resources in this bibliography are here to give you a head start on nearly any aspect of mentoring you want to research.

Articles on Mentoring

Alleman, E. (1982). "Mentoring Relationships in Organizations: Behaviors, Personality Characteristics, and Interpersonal Perceptions." *Dissertation Abstracts International* 43: 75A.

————. (1989). "Two Planned Mentoring Programs that Worked." *Mentoring International* 3 (1): 6-12.

Alleman, E., Cochran, J., Doverspike, J., and Newman, I. (1984). "Enriching Mentoring Relationships." *The Personnel and Guidance Journal* 62 (6): 329-32.

Anderson, E. M., and Shannon, A. L. (1988). "Toward a Conceptualization of Mentoring." *Journal of Teacher Education* 39 (1): 38-42.

Bahniuk, M., Dobos, J., and Hill, S. (1990). "The Impact of Mentoring, Collegial Support, and Information Adequacy on Career Success: A Replication." *Journal of Social Behavior and Personality* 5 (4): 431-51.

Barnett, B. (1990). "The Mentor-Intern Relationship: Making the Most of Learning from Experience." *NASSP Bulletin* 74: 17-24.

Biehl, B. (1992, October). "Mentoring and Discipleship." Paper presented at the National Mentoring Conference, Scottsdale, Arizona.

Bolton, E. (1980). "A Conceptual Analysis of the Mentor Relationship in Career Development of Women." *Adult Education* 30 (4): 195-207.

Borman, C., and Colson, S. (1984). "Mentoring: An Effective Career Guidance Technique." *Vocational Guidance Quarterly* 32 (3): 192-197.

Boston, B. O. (1976). "The Sorcerer's Apprentice: A Case Study in the Role of the Mentor." ERIC Document Reproduction Service No. ED 126 671.

Bova, B. M., and Phillips, R. R. (1981). "The Mentor Relationship: A Study of Mentors and Protégés in Business and Academia." ERIC Document Reproduction Service No. 208 233.

———. (1984). "Mentoring as a Learning Experience for Adults." *Journal of Teacher Education* 35 (3): 16-20.

Bowen, D. (1985). "Were Men Meant to Mentor Women?" *Training and Development Journal* 39 (2): 31-36.

Bruns Schoen, J. (1993). "Mentoring: A Grounded Theory Study from the Perspective of Counselor Educators in Programs Granting Doctorates in Counseling/Counselor." (Doctoral Dissertation, University of South Dakota, 1991). University Microfilms International, 9137440.

Burke, R., and McKeen, C. (1990). "Mentoring in Organizations: Implications for Women." *Journal of Business Ethics* 9: 317-332.

Cahill, M. F., and Kelly, J. J. (1989). "A Mentor Program for Nursing Majors." *Journal of Nursing Education* 28: 40-42.

Cain, R. (1989). "Critical Incidents and Critical Requirements in Mentoring." *Journal of Non-Traditional Studies* 16 (2): 111-127.

Campbell-Heider, N. (1986). "Do Nurses Need Mentors?" *Image: Journal of Nursing Scholarship* 18 (3): 110-113.

Carmin, C. N. (1988). "Issues in Research on Mentoring: Definitional and Methodological." *International Journal of Mentoring* 2 (2): 9-13.

Clawson, J. (1985). "Is Mentoring Necessary?" *Training and Development Journal* 39 (4): 36-39.

Collins, E. G. D., and Scott, P. (1978). "Everyone Who Makes it Has a Mentor." *Harvard Business Review* July-August: 89-101.

Cosgrove, T. (1986). "The Effects of Participation in a Mentoring Transcript Program on College Freshmen." *Journal of College Student Development* 27 (2): 119-124.

Daresh, J. C., Conran, P., and Playko, M. A. (1989). "Mentoring for Leadership Development." ERIC Document Reproduction Service No. ED 304 775.

Darling, L. (1984). "What Do Nurses Want in a Mentor?" *The Journal of Nursing Administration* October: 42-44.

————. (1985a). "Mentor Matching." *The Journal of Nursing Administration* January: 45-46.

————. (1985b). "Mentors and Mentoring." *The Journal of Nursing Administration* March: 42-43.

DeVries, R. C. (1987). "A Description of the Nature and Quality of Assigned Non-Structured Mentoring Relationships in Independent Work Sites." *Dissertation Abstracts International* 49: 405A.

Dreher, G., and Ash, R. (1990). "A Comparative Study of Mentoring Among Men and Women in Managerial, Professional, and Technical Positions." *Journal of Applied Psychology* 75 (5): 539-546.

Erkut, S., and Mokros, J. (1984). "Professors as Models and Mentors for College Students." *American Educational Research Journal* 21 (2): 399-417.

Fagan, M. M., and Walters, G. (1982). "Mentoring Among Teachers." *Journal of Educational Research* 76 (2): 113-117.

Fagenson, F. (1989). "The Mentor Advantage: Perceived Career/Job Experiences of Protégés Versus Non-protégés." *Journal of Organizational Behavior* 10: 309-320.

Fagenson, E. (1992). "Mentoring—Who Needs It? A Comparison of Protégés', and Non-protégés' Needs for Power, Achievement, Affiliation, and Autonomy." *Journal of Vocational Behavior* 41: 48-60.

Farren, C., Gray, J., and Kaye, B. (1984). "Mentoring: A Boon to Career Development." *Personnel Journal* 61 (6): 20-24.

Fitt, L., and Newton, D. (1981). "When the Mentor Is a Man and the Protégé is a Woman." *Harvard Business Review* 59 (2): 56-60.

Frey, B., and Nollar, R. (1986). "Mentoring: A Promise for the Future." *Journal of Creative Behavior* 20 (1): 49-51.

Galvez-Hjornevik, C. (1985). "Mentoring: A Review of the Literature with a Focus on Teaching." ERIC Document Reproduction Service No. ED 262 032.

————. (1986). "Mentoring Among Teachers: A Review of the Literature." *Journal of Teacher Education* 37 (1): 6-11.

Gaskill, L. (1991). "Same-sex and Cross-sex Mentoring of Female Protégés: A Comparative Analysis." *The Career Development Quarterly* 40: 48-63.

Gehrke, N. J. (1988). "On Preserving the Essence of Mentoring as One Form of Teacher Leadership." *Journal of Teacher Education* 39 (1): 43-45.

Gehrke, N., and Kay, R. (1984). "The Socialization of Beginning Teachers through Mentor-protégé Relationships." *Journal of Teacher Education* 35 (3): 21-24.

Hall Daly, Beverly Jean (1987). "Formalized Mentoring Program Model." *Dissertation Abstracts International* 48.

Hamilton, E., Murray, M., Lindholm, L., and Myers, R. (1989). "Effects of Mentoring on Job Satisfaction, Leadership Behaviors, and Job Retention of New Graduate Nurses." *Journal of Nursing Staff Development* July–August: 159-164.

Hamlin, K., and Hering K. (1988). "Help for the First-Year Teacher: Mentor, Buddy, or Both?" *NASSP Bulletin* 72 (509): 125-127.

Haring-Hidore, M. (1987). "Mentoring as a Career Enhancement Strategy for Women." *Journal of Counseling and Development* 66: 147-148.

Horgan, D., and Simeon, R. (1990). "Gender, Mentoring, and Tacit Knowledge." *Journal of Social Behavior and Personality* 5 (4): 453-471.

Howey, K (1988). "Mentor-Teachers as Inquiring Professionals." *Educational Digest* 54 (4): 19-22.

Kram, K. (1983). "Phases of the Mentor Relationship." *Academy of Management Journal* 26 (4): 608-625.

————. (1985). "Improving the Mentoring Process." *Training and*

Development Journal 39 (4): 40-43.

Lageman, A. (1986). "Myths, Metaphors, and Mentors." *Journal of Religion and Health* 25 (1): 58-63.

LeCluyse, Eileen, Tollefson, N., and Borgers, S. (1985). "Differences in Female Graduate Students in Relation to Mentoring." *College Student Journal* 19 (4): 411-415.

Lodge, B. (1989). "Licensed Staff Mentors Likely to Get Hefty Rises." *Times Educational Supplement*, May 12: A1.

McCallum, C. J. (1980). "The Relationship of Perceived Instructional Mentor Influence to Student Educational Development." *Dissertation Abstracts International* 41: 599A.

Merriam, S. (1983). "Mentors and Protégés: A Critical Review of the Literature." *Adult Education Quarterly* 33 (3): 161-73.

Moore, K. M. (1982). "The Role of Mentors in Developing Leaders for Academe." *Educational Record* 63 (1): 23-28.

Moore, K. M., and Salimbene, A. M. (1983). "The Dynamics of the Mentor-Protégé Relationship in Developing Women as Academic Leaders." *Journal of Educational Equity and Leadership* 2 (1): 51-64.

Noller, R. (1982). "Mentoring: A Renaissance of Apprenticeship." *Journal of Creative Behavior* 16 (1): 1-4.

Phillips-Jones, L. (1983). "Establishing a Formalized Mentoring Program." *Training and Development Journal* 37 (2): 38-42.

Ragins, B., and Cotton, J. (1991). "Easier Said than Done: Gender Differences in Perceived Barriers to Gaining a Mentor." *Academy of Management Journal* 34 (4): 939-951.

Rawlins, M., and Rawlins, L. (1983). "Mentoring and Networking for Helping Professionals." *Personnel and Guidance Journal* 62 (2): 116-118.

Roche, G. (1979). "Much Ado About Mentors." *Harvard Business Review* 57 (1): 14-28.

Runkel, T. E. (1982). "The Role of Mentors in the Career Development of Ministers." *Dissertation Abstracts International* 43: 2561A.

Sands, R., Parson, L., and Duane, J. (1991). "Faculty Mentoring Faculty in a Public University." *Journal of Higher Education* 62 (2): 174-193.

Scandura, T. (1992). "Mentorship and Career Mobility: An Empirical

203

Investigation." *Journal of Organizational Behavior* 13: 169-174.

Schmidt, J., and Wolfe, J. (1980). "The Mentor Partnership: Discovery of Professionalism." *NASPA Journal* 17 (3): 45-51.

Scott, M. (1992). "Designing Effective Mentoring Programs: Historical Perspectives and Current Issues." *Journal of Humanistic Education and Development* 30: 167-177.

Serlen, B. (1989). "How Mentoring Programs Work." *Journal of Career Planning and Employment* 49: 54-56.

Shandley, T. C. (1989). "The Use of Mentors for Leadership Development." *NASPA Journal* 27 (1): 59-66.

Shapiro, F., Haseltine, F, and Rowe, M. (1978). "Moving Up: Role Models, Mentors, and the Patron System." *Sloan Management Review* 19: 51-58.

Sullivan, R., and Miklas, D. (1985). "On-the-job Training that Works." *Training and Development Journal* 39 (5): 118-120.

Swerklik, M., and Bardon, J. (1988). "A Survey of Mentoring Experiences in School Psychology." *The Journal of School Psychology* 26: 213-224.

Terrell, M., Hassell, R., and Duggar, M. (1992). "Mentoring Programs: a Blueprint for Personal Growth and Academic Development." *National Association of Student Personnel Administration Journal* 29 (3): 199-206.

Whitely, W., Dougherty, T., and Dreher, G. (1991). "Relationship of Career Mentoring and Social Economic Origin to Manager's and Professional's Early Career Progress." *Academy of Management Journal* 34 (2): 331-351.

Whitely, W., Dougherty, T., and Dreher, G. (1992). "Correlates of Career Oriented Mentoring for Early Career Managers and Professionals." *Journal of Organizational Behavior* 13: 141-154.

Willbur, J. (1987). "Does Mentoring Breed Success?" *Training and Development Journal* 41 (11): 38- 41.

Wilde, J., and Schau, C. (1991). "Mentoring in Graduate Schools of Education: Mentee's Perceptions." *Journal of Experimental Education* 59 (2): 165-179.

Woodlands Group, (1980). "Management Development Roles: Coach, Sponsor, and Mentor." *Personnel Journal* 59 (11): 918-921.

Zey, M. (1985). "Mentor Programs: Making the Right Moves."

Personnel Journal 64 (2): 53-57.

Books on Mentoring

Alleman, E. (1986). "Measuring Mentoring—Frequency, Quality, Impact." In *Proceedings of the First International Conference on Mentoring*, vol. 2., ed. W. A. Gray and M. M. Gray. Vancouver, British Columbia, Canada: International Association for Mentoring, 44-51.

Anderson, R., and Ramey, P. (1990). "Women in Higher Education: Development through Administrative Mentoring." In *Women in Higher Education—Changes and Challenges*, ed. L. Welch. New York: Praeger, 183-190.

Appel, M., and Trail, T. (1986). "Building Effective Professional Adult Education Mentoring." In *Proceedings of the First International Conference on Mentoring*, vol. 1., ed. W. A. Gray and M. M. Gray. Vancouver, British Columbia, Canada: International Association for Mentoring, 63-70.

Baack, J. (1982). "Evaluation of Mentoring Transcript Programs." In *Mentoring-transcript Systems for Promoting Student Growth*, ed. R. Brown and D. DeCoster. San Francisco: Jossey-Bass, 79-90.

Biehl, B., and Urquhart, G. (1990). *Mentoring: How to Find a Mentor, How to Be One.* Laguna Niguel, CA: Masterplanning Group.

Bradshaw, L. (1992). "Evaluating Success in High Risk Student Mentor Programs." In *Proceedings of the International Mentoring Association*, Chicago, IL. Kalamazoo: Western Michigan University Press, 95-101.

Caruso, R. (1992). *Mentoring and the Business Environment—Asset or Liability?* Brookfield, VT: Dartmouth Publishing Company.

Chiogioji, E. and Pritz, S. (1992). "Mentoring to Support the Mission of a Government Agency." In *Proceedings of the International Mentoring Association*, Chicago, IL. Kalamazoo: Western Michigan University Press, 288-296.

Clawson, J. (1980). "Mentoring in Managerial Careers." In *Work, Family, and the Career: New Frontiers in Theory and Research*, ed. C. Derr. New York: Praeger, 144-165.

Clinton, J., and Clinton, R. (1991). *The Mentor Handbook: Detailed*

Guidelines and Helps for Christian Mentors and Mentorees. Altadena, CA: Barnabas Publishers.

Collin, A. (1986). "The Role of the Mentor in the Experience of Change." In *Proceedings of the First International Conference on Mentoring*, vol. 2., ed. W. A. Gray and M. M. Gray. Vancouver, British Columbia, Canada: International Association for Mentoring, 94-101.

Covington, R. (1992). "Talented and Ten: The Peer Mentor Program at North Carolina State University." In *Proceedings of the International Mentoring Association*, Chicago, IL. Kalamazoo: Western Michigan University Press.

Daloz, L. A. (1986). *Effective Teaching and Mentoring.* San Francisco: Jossey-Bass Publishers.

Egan, J. B. (1986). "Characteristics of Mentor Teachers' Mentor-Protégé Relationships." In *Proceedings of the First International Conference on Mentoring*, vol. 1., ed. W. A. Gray and M. M. Gray. Vancouver, British Columbia, Canada: International Association for Mentoring, 55-62.

Enz, R., Anderson, G., Weber, B., and Lawhead, D. (1992). "The Arizona Teacher Residency Program: Commitment, Collaboration, and Collegiality." In *Teacher Induction and Mentoring—School-based Collaborative Programs*, ed. G. Debolt. Albany: State University of New York Press, 97-118.

Fagan, M. M. (1986). "Do Formal Mentoring Programs Really Mentor?" In *Proceedings of the First International Conference on Mentoring*, vol. 2., ed. W. A. Gray and M. M. Gray. Vancouver, British Columbia, Canada: International Association for Mentoring, 23-43.

Garcia, M. (1992). "Mentoring the New Graduate at JPL." In *Proceedings of the International Mentoring Association*, Chicago, IL. Kalamazoo: Western Michigan University Press, 162-171.

Gray, W. A. (1986). Components for Developing a Successful Formalized Mentoring Program in Business, the Professions, and Other Settings. In *Proceedings of the First International Conference on Mentoring*, vol. 2., ed. W. A. Gray and M. M. Gray. Vancouver, British Columbia, Canada: International Association for Mentoring, 15-22.

Gray, W. A., and Gray, M. M., eds. (1986). *Mentoring: A Comprehensive Annotated Bibliography of Important References.* Vancouver, British Columbia, Canada: International Association for Mentoring.

Green, D., and McLauchlin, R. (1992). Fayetteville State University's Pilot Mentoring Program. In *Proceedings of the International Mentoring Association*, Chicago, IL. Kalamazoo: Western Michigan University Press, 172-180.

Haensly, P. A., and Edlind, E. P. (1986). A Search for Ideal Types in Mentoring. In *Proceedings of the First International Conference on Mentoring*, vol. 1., ed. W. A. Gray and M. M. Gray. Vancouver, British Columbia, Canada: International Association for Mentoring, 1-8.

Hunt, D. A. (1986). "Formal Vs. Informal Mentoring: Toward a Framework." In *Proceedings of the First International Conference on Mentoring*, vol. 2., ed. W. A. Gray and M. M. Gray. Vancouver, British Columbia, Canada: International Association for Mentoring, 8-14.

Kram, K. (1986). "Mentoring in the Workplace." In *Career Development in Organizations*, ed. D. Hall and Associates. San Francisco: Jossey-Bass, 160-201.

———. (1988). *Mentoring at Work: Developmental Relationships in Organizational Life.* Lanham, MD: University Press of America.

Milan, C. (1990). "The Learning Autobiography: A Foundation for Mentoring." In *New Directions for Adult and Continuing Education.* San Francisco: Jossey Bass, 59-63.

Murray, M. (1991). *Beyond the Myths and Magic of Mentoring: How to Facilitate an Effective Mentoring Program.* San Francisco: Jossey-Bass.

Phillips-Jones, L. (1982). *Mentors and Protégés.* New York: Arbor House.

Spruance, F. (1992). *Mentoring Manual.* Dresher, PA: Conservative Baptist Seminary of the East.

Stanley, P., and Clinton, J. (1992). *Connecting: The Mentoring Relationships You Need to Succeed in Life.* Colorado Springs: NavPress.

Tate, V., and Lew, J. (1992). Mentoring a Diverse Workforce. In *Proceedings of the International Mentoring Association*, Chicago,

IL. Kalamazoo: Western Michigan University Press, 490-93.

Torrance, P. (1984). *Mentor Relationships: How They Aid Creative Achievement, Endure, Change, and Die.* Buffalo, NY: Bearly Limited.

Zey, M. C. (1986). "Only the Beginning: Five Major Trends that Signal the Growth of Corporate Formal Mentor Programs." In *Proceedings of the First International Conference on Mentoring,* vol. 2., ed. W. A. Gray and M. M. Gray. Vancouver, British Columbia, Canada: International Association for Mentoring, 153-60.

Zey, M. (1991). *The Mentor Connection: Strategic Alliances in Corporate Life.* New Brunswick: Transaction Publishers.

Other Resource Information on Mentoring

Alleman, E. (1991). "Managing Mentoring Relationships in Organizations." College Industry Education Conference. San Diego: California.

Blackwell, J. E (1989). "Mentoring: An Action Strategy for Increasing Minority Faculty." *Academe* 75 (5): 8-14.

Bower, A., and Younger, G. (1989). "Mentor-Intern Relationships in New York State's Formal Program: Beginnings." *Action in Teacher Education* 11 (2): 60-65.

Burke, R. (1984). "Mentors in Organizations." *Group and Organizational Studies* 9 (3): 353-72.

Carden, A. (1990). "Mentoring and Adult Career Development: the Evolution of a Theory." *The Counseling Psychologist* 18 (2): 275-299.

Castor, L. L. (1987). "Mentoring: An Analysis of Facilitators, Barriers and Alternatives." *Dissertation Abstracts International* 48: 2549A-2550A.

Cesa, I., and Fraser, S. (1989). "A Method for Encouraging the Development of Good Mentor-protégé Relationships." *Teaching of Psychology* 16 (3): 125-28.

Clemson, R. (1987). "Mentoring in Teaching." *Action in Teacher Education* 9 (3): 85-90.

Cronan-Hillix, T., Gensheimer, L., Cronan-Hillix, W., and Davidson, W. (1986). "Student's Views of Mentors in Psychology Graduate

Training." *Teaching of Psychology* 13 (3): 123-27.

Daloz, L. A. (1983). "Mentors: Teachers who Make a Difference." *Change* 15 (6): 24-27.

Daloz, L. A. (1987). "Martha Meets Her Mentor: The Power of Teaching Relationships." *Change* 19 (6): 35-37.

Daresh, J., and Playko, M. (1989). "Teacher Mentors and Administrator Mentors: Same Track, Different Trains." *Planning and Changing* 20: 88-96.

Galbraith, L., Brueggemeyer, A., and Manweiler, D. (1988). "Failure to Flourish: Indications for Mentoring." *Pediatric Nursing* 14 (5): 405-8.

Gehrke, N. (1988b). "Toward a Definition of Mentoring." *Theory Into Practice* 27 (3): 190-95.

Gray, W., and Gray, M. (1985). "Synthesis of Research on Mentoring Beginning Teachers." *Educational Leadership* 43 (3): 37-43.

Hardcastle, B. (1989). "Spiritual Connections: Protégés' Reflections on Significant Mentorships." *Theory into Practice* 27 (3): 201-8.

Head, F., Reiman, A., and Thies-Sprinthall, R. (1992). "The Reality of Mentoring: Complexity on its Process and Function." In *Mentoring—Contemporary Principles and Issues*, ed. T. Bey and C. Holmes. Reston, VA: Association of Teacher Education, 5-24.

Healy, C., and Welchert, A. (1990). "Mentoring Relationships: A Definition to Advance Research and Practice." *Educational Researcher* 19: 17-21.

Henning, J. (1984). "The Lawyer as Mentor and Supervisor." *Legal Economics* Sept.-Oct.: 19-24.

Hill, S., Bahniuk, M., and Dobos, J. (1989). "The Impact of Mentoring and Collegial Support on Faculty Success: An Analysis of Support Behavior, Information Adequacy, and Communication Apprehension." *Communication Education* 38: 15-33.

Hill, S., Bahniuk, M., Dobos, J., and Rouner, D. (1989). "Mentoring and Other Communication Support in the Academic Setting." *Group and Organizational Studies* 14 (3): 355-68.

Hunt, D. A., and Michael, C. (1983). "Mentorship: A Career Training and Development Tool." *Academy of Management Review* 8 (3): 475-85.

Irvine, J. (1986). "The Master Teacher as Mentor: Role Perceptions of

Beginning and Master Teachers." *Education* 106 (2): 123-30.

Johnsrud, L. (1990). "Mentor Relationships: Those that Help and Those that Hinder." *New Directions for Higher Education* 72: 57-66.

Johnsrud, L. (1991). "Mentoring Between Academic Women: The Capacity for Interdependence." *Initiatives* 54: 7-17.

Kinsey, D. (1990). "Mentorship and Influence in Nursing." *Nursing Management* 21 (5): 45-46.

Klug, B., and Salzman, S. (1991). "Formal Induction vs. Informal Mentoring: Comparative Effects and Outcomes." *Teaching and Teacher Education* 7 (3): 241-51.

Kram, K., and Bragar, M. (1992). "Development through Mentoring: A Strategic Approach." In *Career Development: Theory and Practice*, ed. D. Montross and C. Shinkman. Springfield, Illinois: Charles C. Thomas, 221-54.

Kram, K., and Hall, D. (1989). "Mentoring as an Antidote to Stress During Corporate Trauma." *Human Resource Management* 28 (4): 493-510.

Lambert, D., and Lambert, L. (1985). "Mentor Teachers as Change Facilitators." *Thrust* April-May: 28-32.

Lindholm, J. (1982). "Mentoring: The Mentor's Perspective." Technical Report No. 9. Cambridge, MA: Massachusetts Institute of Technology, Sloan School of Management.

Little, J. (1988). "The Mentor Phenomenon and the Social Organization of Teaching." *Review of Research in Education* 16: 297-351.

Merriam, S. (1983). "Mentors and Protégés: A Critical Review." *Adult Education Quarterly* 33 (3): 161-73.

Moore, K. (1982). "The Role of Mentors in Developing Leaders for Academe." *Educational Record* winter: 23-28.

Noe, R. (1988). "Women and Mentoring: A Review and Research Agenda." *Academy of Management Review* 13 (1): 65-78.

Odiorne, G. (1985). "Mentoring: An American Management Innovation." *Personnel Administrator* 30 (5): 63-70.

Orth, C., Wilkinson, H., and Benfari, R. (1987). "The Manager as Coach and Mentor." *Organizational Dynamics* spring: 66-74.

Parkay, F. (1988). "Reflections of a Protégé." *Theory Into Practice* 27 (3): 195-200.

Ragins, B. (1989). "Barriers to Mentoring: The Female Manager's

Dilemma." *Human Relations* 42 (1): 1-22.

Schockett, M., and Haring-Hidore, M. (1985). "Factor Analytic Support for Psychosocial and Vocational Mentoring Functions." *Psychological Reports* 57: 627-30.

Stalker, J. (1992, November). "Athene in Academe: Women Mentoring Women in the Academy." Paper presented at a Joint Conference of the Australian Association for Research in Education and the New Zealand Association for Research in Education, Geelong, Australia.

Stalker, J. (1993, May). "Women Teachers Mentoring Women Learners: On the Inside Working it Out." In *Proceedings of the 34th Annual Adult Education Research Conference*, ed. D. Flannery. University Park, PA: Penn State University, 269-74.

Stroble, E., and Cooper J. M. (1988). "Mentor Teachers: Coaches or Referees?" *Theory into Practice* 27 (3): 231-36.

Van Zandt, C., and Perry, N. (1992). "Helping the Rookie School Counselor: A Mentoring Project." *The School Counselor* 39: 159-63.

Wagner, L. (1985). "Ambiguities and Possibilities in California's Mentor Teacher Program." *Educational Leadership* 43 (3): 23-29.

Weber, C. E. (1980). "Mentoring." *Directors and Boards* 5 (3): 17-24.

Wright, C., and Wright, S. (1987). "The Role of Mentors in the Career Development of Young Professionals." *Family Relations* 36: 204-8.

Yamamoto, K. (1988). "To See Life Grow: The Meaning of Mentorship." *Theory Into Practice* 27 (3): 181-89.

Zey, M. C. (1984). *The Mentor Connection*. Homewood, IL: Dow Jones-Irvin.

Zimpher, N. L., and Rieger, S. R. (1988). "Mentoring Teachers: What Are the Issues?" *Theory into Practice* 27 (3): 175-82.

Protégé "Getting to Know You" Questionnaire

The two worksheets in this appendix help you and your mentor or protégé agree on relational boundaries and get to know each other before or at the beginning of a mentoring relationship. These worksheet are printed on their own pages to facilitate photocopying.

Clarifying Expectations Before Entering A Mentoring Relationship

1. How much time do the mentor and protégé plan to be together?

_____

2. Will money be loaned? _____

3. What are the specific needs the protégé feels at this time?

_____

_____

_____

_____

_____

4. Ideally, how many years do the mentor and protégé expect this relationship to last? _____

5. Are there any limits the mentor or protégé want to establish?

_____

_____

_____

_____

_____

_____

6. What are the mentor and protégé's assumptions and expectations about the nature of this relationship?

_____

_____

_____

_____

_____

7. Has either the mentor or the protégé experienced failed or disappointing mentoring relationships? Are there any outstanding issues that may have caused the failure?

_____

_____

_____

_____

_____

8. Do the mentor or protégé expect each other to be perfect? If so, this must be discussed now! _____

9. What anxieties, uncertainties, uneasiness, and inadequacies does the mentor or protégé feel about this relationship?

_____

_____

_____

_____

_____

_____

Protégé "Getting to Know You" Questionnaire

This is an optional series of questions a mentor can ask a protégé in the getting acquainted process . . . .any order is fine . . . skip any you like!

What do you see as your top three strengths in rank order?

1. _____

2. _____

3. _____

What ten specific measurable things do you want to get done before age sixty-five?

1. _____

2. _____

3. _____

4. _____

5. _____

6. _____

7. _____

8. _____

9. _____

10. _____

What do you consider your lifework? _____

What are your three deepest personal needs which make you potentially vulnerable . . . morally, ethically or legally?

1. _____

2. _____

3. _____

Which three people threaten you most personally? Why?

1. _____

2. _____

3. _____

Who are the three people who are (or could be) your mentors?

1. _____

2. _____

3. _____

Who are three people who could be your protégés?

1. _____

2. _____

3. _____

What is your "preferred ideal hope-to-have-someday" title (president, guru, teacher, friend, etc.)? _____

217

What three things would you most like to change about yourself if you could? Why?

1._____

2._____

3._____

What three things are you most committed to doing before you die?

1._____

2._____

3._____

What three things do you feel are your greatest roadblocks in your life at this point?

1._____

2._____

3._____

In what three areas would you most like to grow personally in the next one to five years?

1._____

2._____

3._____

What one to three things are keeping you from being as close to God as you would like?

1._____

2._____

3._____

How do you picture yourself in ten years, ideally? _____

_____

_____

What one subject would you most like to share from your heart of hearts that you have never been able to put into words? _____

_____

What have been your life's:
Milestones? _____

_____

_____

_____

_____

Traumas? _____

_____

_____

_____

_____

_____

Questions? _____

_____

_____

_____

_____

How would you describe your general style of leading?_____

_____

_____

_____

How would you describe your relationship with each of your
immediate family members when you were growing up? _____

_____

_____

What three relational bridges do you need/want to rebuild?

1._____

2._____

3._____

Who are your five closest friends? Why?

1._____

2._____

3._____

4._____

5._____

Free forum—Anything else you would like to share on any subject!

_____

_____

_____

_____

Questions to Ask to Help Your Protégé Define Her/His Dream
AND A PRACTICAL PLAN TO TURN THE DREAM INTO REALITY

The primary reason for writing this book was to increase your confidence as a mentor. One of the ways to do that, as I mentioned earlier, is to increase the predictability of mentoring so that no matter what happens, you know what to do next.

One of the topics that will come up again and again as you mentor younger, less-experienced people is the question of focus, of putting life into focus, or refocusing life.

Below, you will find some of the most helpful questions I've been able to develop/collect in the last twenty years for the focusing and refocusing of dreams and plans. When a protégé comes to you and expresses frustration with a lack of focus, you should be able to confidently say to her/him, "I know exactly what you need. Hold on, let me go get a few questions to ask you which will help you focus or refocus at this point."

For the next few hours, you can either discuss the questions or let them write out answers and bring them back to you. It will not be long before you find focus returning to your protégé's life.

DREAMING . . . about the Future in a Practical Way

These are some of my very favorite questions, collected over the past twenty years. Each has proven very trustworthy.

1. God: What three changes in me would most please our Eternal God in His Holy Heaven?

2. Dream/Purpose: What can I do to make the most significant difference for God in my lifetime? Why am I on the earth? What is the very best organizational context for my dream?

3. Primary Result: What is the single best measurable indicator that I am making progress toward my dream?

4. Life Priorities: If I could accomplish only three measurable priorities before I die, what would I accomplish?

5. Ten-Year Focus: If I could accomplish only three measurable priorities in the next ten years that would make a fifty percent difference in my lifelong contribution, what would I accomplish?

6. Annual Focus:
   Single-Word Focus
   > What single word best captures the focus of my next year?

   Opportunity
   > Where was my greatest unexpected success last year? Why? What three steps could I take now to take full advantage of this "Window of Opportunity" this coming year?

   Land Mines
   > What three land mines or roadblocks need my immediate attention? What have I been praying most about in the past thirty days? What three changes could reduce my "risk" by fifty percent?

3/10/50%
> If I could only accomplish three measurable priorities in the
> next twelve months that would make a fifty percent
> difference in my contribution in the next ten years,
> which three things would I most want to accomplish?

7. Quarterly Focus: What three measurable priorities could I accomplish in the next ninety days to make a fifty percent difference in the results I see by the end of the year?

8. Organization: What three changes could I make to see a fifty percent difference in our morale as a family or team?

9. Cash: If I had to cut my budget twenty-one percent, what would be the first three things to go? If I got a surprise gift of twenty-one percent of my budget, what three things would I do immediately?

10. Quality: What three changes could improve the quality of my work by fifty percent in the next twelve months?

Helping You Win

Additional field-tested resources

Asking To Win!
Helpful 24 x 7 x 365 x life!

This booklet fits into your suit coat pocket, purse, or briefcase. It contains over one hundred profound questions to help you make wise decisions twenty-four hours a day, seven days a week, for the rest of your life. Would you benefit from knowing how to ask penetrating, powerful, practical questions? Would you like to be able to ask exactly the "right questions" at the "right time"? This booklet works.

Board Member, (The) Effective
by Bobb Biehl and Ted W. Engstrom

This one book turns boardroom anxiety, confusion, and frustration into . . . BOARDROOM CONFIDENCE!

Have you ever wished you could sit down and chat with a mentor who would help you be more confident and effective in your position on the board?

In *The Effective Board Member*, you now have available two seasoned boardroom veterans (with combined experience with over one hundred boards), eager to help you! This book is extremely helpful if you:

- Are trying to choose the right board members
- Serve on a board
- Need to make board presentations
- Are trying to decide whether to accept a board position
- Are new to a board

• Have been a board member a long while, but have never had any formal board training

Quantity discounts available so each member of your board can have her or his own copy.

Building Your First Church Building . . . Successfully!
Get his experience on your side—before you build.

Joe Kimbel has over forty years of experience in church design and construction and has been involved in building over one thousand church buildings. He has pastored several churches and been a district superintendent.

Joe takes you through the step-by-step process of building a church building. He shares stories, illustrations, rules-of-thumb, warnings, and encouragement that one would expect from a loving father or a caring mentor.

Whatever you do, if you are about to build—especially if you are feeling a bit shaky—GET THIS RESOURCE!

Career Change/LifeWork
30 Questions to Ask Before Making Any Major Career Change

Is your current position "just a job," your next "career move," or your "lifework"?

This series of thirty questions comes in handy any time you are thinking about the possibility of making a work change. If you are uncertain, these profoundly simple ideas can help. You can also help friends in transition. You hand them the thirty questions; they may take hours to answer the questions, but they will come back with well-thought-out answers. These questions save hours of time in decision making.

Helpful in any career re-evaluating process between the ages of twenty-five to sixty. A proven resource!

226

Dream Energy
Have you got all of the natural energy you would like?

There are many forms of energy . . . solar energy, caloric energy, caffeine energy, social energy, electrical energy, etc. One of the most powerful forms of energy is "DREAM ENERGY"!

With a clear dream, getting up early, working hard all day, and going to bed late is "easy." Without a clear dream, we tend to sleep as late as possible, drag our way through the day, and flop into bed as soon as possible. This new book helps you define your life dream and as a result gives you a major increase in the amount of your "DREAM ENERGY"!

At the same time, a team without a dream is not a team at all . . . it is a group of individuals in the "same uniform." It takes a dream for any team to move beyond petty ego trips and pull together for the sake of turning a team dream into reality.

Event Planning Checklist
by Ed Trenner

This comprehensive THREE-HUNDRED-POINT CHECK LIST can cut your planning time in half, especially if you are new to "special events."

This checklist is designed for those who receive great pleasure from precision and for those who have yet to experience it. The three-hundred-point check list helps you keep from overlooking an obvious question and finding "egg-on-your-face" at the event. Practical, proven, easy-to-use.

Focusing By Asking
Drive time CD

Profound questions have helped thousands of people, in all walks of life, at all levels of leadership, focus their lives and teams. This drive-time series is set up with five-minute tracks, covering the following ten critical elements of leadership:

PERSONAL FOCUS –
    Keeping FOCUSED
    Keeping CONFIDENT
    Keeping BALANCED
    Keeping MOTIVATED
    Keeping ORGANIZED

TEAM FOCUS –
    Master ASKING
    Master COMMUNICATING
    Master LEADING
    Master MOTIVATING
    Master PLANNING

Whenever you need to see things in crystal-clear focus, remember to pop in this drive-time CD or cassette tape.

Fourth Grade
The single most shaping year of a human being's existence

This tape was created for anyone who cares about fourth graders — or for anyone with younger children who will soon be in the fourth grade (listed alphabetically).
    • Christian education directors
    • Elementary Sunday school teachers
    • Elementary school teachers
    • Grandparents
    • Home schoolers

- Little League coaches
- Parents
- Psychologists and other counselors
- Senior pastors

On this video you will learn why the fourth grade is so extremely shaping, how to take advantage of this very narrow window of opportunity with your fourth grader, and how to avoid serious damage in this highly impressionable period of life. You will understand how at least ten of your leadership "comfort zones" were established in the fourth grade and how to use this information to help you find a role in life that "fits" you!

It is impossible to overstate the importance of this one tape if you deal with fourth graders—and it's also an ideal gift for any person you know who does, including any professional from the above list who has a major influence in the shaping of your fourth grader.

LEADING with Confidence

Approximately four thousand people have completed the (30 Days to) Confident Leadership (formerly titled Leadership Confidence) series. A wise, proven investment in your own future, this series is a life-long leadership reference covering thirty essential leadership areas, including:

- HOW TO COPE WITH— Change, Depression, Failure, Fatigue, Pressure
- HOW TO BECOME MORE— Attractive, Balanced, Confident, Creative, Disciplined, Motivated
- HOW TO DEVELOP SKILLS IN—Asking, Dreaming, Goal Setting, Prioritizing, Risk Taking, Influencing, Money Managing, Personal Organization, Problem Solving, Decision Making, Communicating
- HOW TO BECOME MORE EFFECTIVE IN—Delegating, Firing, Reporting, Team Building, People Building, Recruiting, Masterplanning, Motivating

Masterplanning–Arrow

Masterplanning Arrow (24" x 36") helps you and your team quickly see:

THE "BIG PICTURE" . . . when you are drowning in detail
THE "FOREST" . . . when you feel lost in the trees
THE "SYMPHONY" . . . not just a few notes

The Masterplanning Arrow teaches you how to quickly sort out the direction of any organization, division, department, or major project you ever lead anywhere, at any time, for the rest of your life. The Arrow is now available with easy to follow step-by-step instructions on the back, even if you do not order the book or tape series.

Masterplanning–Book

This series presents the same track the Masterplanning Group has refined in day-to-day consulting practice for over twenty-five years to help clients develop their Masterplans.

THE PROCESS HAS BEEN USED SUCCESSFULLY:
From mom and pop organizations to a staff of thousands
From start-up budgets to hundreds of millions a year
From local churches to international organizations in over
one hundred countries
From small local churches (fifty) to large area churches
(four thousand or more)
From those with no business experience to Harvard MBAs

PREDICTABLE SYMPTOMS WITHOUT A MASTERPLAN
A Masterplan can be likened to a musical score for a symphony orchestra. "Unless everyone's on the same sheet of music, the result will not be pleasant to the ears." Without a Masterplan, expect the following:

1. DIRECTIONAL COMMUNICATIONS (internal and external) are foggy.
2. FRUSTRATION, TENSION, and PRESSURE develop because of differing assumptions.
3. DECISION MAKING is POSTPONED because a FRAMEWORK is not available for clear decisions.
4. ENERGY and RESOURCES ARE WASTED because the basic systems are not clearly developed.
5. FUNDING is INADEQUATE because of a lack of consistent communication to the organization's constituency.
6. The ORGANIZATION SUFFERS because the creative energies are spent putting out fires.

It is helpful to have a clear Masterplan.

Memories Book

Are your parents, grandparents, favorite aunts and uncles, or mentors still living?

Then *Memories* is an ideal gift. Written memories become family heirlooms for your children's children and are guaranteed to become priceless with the passage of time.

Memories contains over five hundred memory-jogging questions to help your loved one relive and write about her or his life's milestones. It's a beautiful album-type book with padded covers and a binding which opens widely for easy writing.

Memories is also a "boomerang" gift! You give it to your loved one this year, he or she fills it with memories over the next one to fifty years, then it returns to you as an heirloom for your children's children.

Mentoring
How to Find a Mentor and How to Become One

A mentoring relationship can easily add a feeling of thirty to fifty percent extra LIFE-LEADERSHIP HORSEPOWER to any person. Without a mentor, a person often feels underpowered, as if not living up to her or his true potential.

This powerful resource gives you very useful steps about forming a mentoring relationship and answers practical mentoring questions with proven answers.

Mid-life Storm
Avoiding a "Mid-Life Crisis"

This hope-filled book contains a crystal-clear "Mid-Life Map," which helps guide you or a friend successfully through the very dangerous mid-life years.

Just because you or your mate is beginning to ask a few mid-life questions does not automatically mean you are experiencing the dreaded "Mid-Life Crisis." There are three distinctly different mid-life phases:
- Mid-Life Re-evaluation
- Mid-Life Crisis
- Mid-Life Drop Out

This book addresses each of the three phases with specific step-by-step instructions on how to avoid the pain and confusion of a mid-life crisis— or if you are already there, how to get out and get on with the rest of your life.

On My Own
An ideal graduation gift!

Many adults have said that they wish their parents had taught them these principles before they started off "on their own." Parents, as well as students, benefit from these extremely fundamental leadership principles.

If you have been increasingly concerned about your high school or college student's readiness to face the "real world," this book has been written for your son or daughter.

These principles will stay with your son or daughter for a lifetime. And they can pass them on to their children's children.

Pre-Marriage: Getting To "Really Know" Your Life Mate-To-Be
Pre-marriage Questions

These are the heart-to-heart questions you ask before you say "I Do" to make sure this is the right person for you. It is hard to break up any relationship, but it is far better to break an engagement than a marriage. Most couples find that they have far more in common than they had even realized. The handful of major disagreements can be discussed before marriage to see if they are major differences which are "engagement breakers" or if they are just uncomfortable differences.

If you have any doubts at all about your upcoming marriage—and just want to make sure this is the life mate for you—this book can help! A very appropriate pre-marriage gift for any friend.

Presidential Profile

- How would you rate your current president—on the thirty dimensions required to be a world-class president?
- Which of the candidates you are interviewing to be our next president gets the highest rating on the thirty-point presidential profile?
- Are you out to be a president? Should you let your name stand? How would you rate yourself as a president on these thirty leadership dimensions?
- Where do you need to grow to be ready to be president—someday?

If you have been asking yourself any of the above presidential questions, this easy-to-understand (1-10 scale) profile can be a proven guide for your reflections and your team's discussions and evaluations.

Staff Evaluation–135

Have you ever wanted a comprehensive evaluation checklist for telling a staff member exactly how he or she is doing, on a 1-10 scale, in everything from bad breath to decision making?

This is an ideal annual tool for you to use with those close to you, focusing on one hundred thirty-five dimensions in all. Furthermore, if you'd like, let them evaluate you. This list helps maximize your staff evaluation and communication ability, while concentrating on the positive.

Stop Setting Goals

Do you hate setting goals—or know someone who does?

Then this book is for you! The most common reaction to this book is: "I no longer feel like a second-class citizen!" This simple paradigm shift has already freed thousands of readers for life!

As a team leader, you can reduce team tensions and, at the same time, significantly increase team spirit by introducing this simple idea at your next staff meeting.

Strategy Work Sheets
(11" x 17")

A quick, systematic, step-by-step method to think through a solid success strategy for each of your goals. Use these sheets to ask each staff member to draft a strategy for turning each major goal into a realistic plan. *Strategy Work Sheets* help you spot problems in basic thinking and strategy before those problems become costly. Includes twenty-four sheets for use with your team.

234

Team Profile
"What makes you tick?" "What turns you on?" "What burns you out?"

The *Team Profile* is a proven (7th edition—18th printing since 1980) way of understanding yourself better. In simple language, it lets you tell your spouse, your friends, or your colleagues what makes you "tick." *Team Profile* clarifies what you really want to do, not what you have to do, have done the most, or think others expect of you. It is the key to understanding personal fulfillment and is an affordable way of building strong team unity by predicting team chemistry. This profoundly simple, self-scoring, self-interpreting inventory is the key to selecting the right person for the right position, thus helping avoid costly hiring mistakes.

Why You Do What You Do
4th Printing

This book is a result of over forty thousand hours of behind-the-defenses experiences with some of the finest, emotionally healthy leaders of our generation. This model was developed to maximize "healthy" people with a few emotional "mysteries" still unanswered!

Why do I have a phobic fear of failure, rejection, or insignificance? Why am I so "driven" to be admired, recognized, appreciated, secure, respected, or accepted? Why am I an enabler, leader, promoter, rescuer, controller, people pleaser? Why am I a perfectionist, workaholic? Why are pastors vulnerable to affairs? Where am I the most vulnerable to temptation? How do I guard against temptation? Why do I have such a hard time relating to my parents when I love them so much? Why do they sometimes seem like such children?

These and other "emotional mysteries" can be understood and resolved in the silence of your own heart without years of therapy.

Widow's Workbook (The), A Widow's Bible Study
By Dixie Johnston Fraley Keller

Dixie Johnston Fraley Keller was widowed while people watched, on television, a "Lear jet that was out of control." Metaphorically, as life with her husband was soaring, her world all came crashing down.

As she has picked up the pieces, she invites you to join her widow's walk down this winding road. Learn to live from death in the following areas:
- Loving and losing
- Appreciating
- Coping
- Giving
- Grieving
- Living on

If you are a widow, or know someone who is, this gift can help on the lonely road of recovery.

Writing Your First Book!
Bobb Biehl and Mary Beshear, Ph.D.

If you have been wanting to write a book for years, but still haven't finished a manuscript, let *Writing Your First Book!* be your starting point! This is a skeleton outline—no complicated, sophisticated theory, or double talk. It is just a bare bones, easy-to-follow, step-by-step checklist to become a royalty-receiving author. A wise investment in your own future.

APPENDIX E

QuickWisdom.com

AN INTRODUCTION . . . AND AN INVITATION!

As an executive mentor/consultant, I have the rare privilege of spending days at a time with some of the finest leaders of our generation. I continue to grow personally, learning more in the past year than I've learned in the five years before it.

Mentoring Realities

In my book *Mentoring*, I define mentoring ideally as "a lifelong relationship in which the mentor helps the protege grow into her/his God-given potential over a lifetime." Realistically, because of schedule pressures, my personal mentoring is limited to a very few individuals. At the same time, I truly want to see friends like you grow into your God-given potential over your lifetime.

Solomon advised, "Get Wisdom."

The search of today seems to be focused on becoming a courageous, charming, powerful, successful person. However, according to the Bible, Solomon, who was one of the wisest, if not the wisest, man that ever lived, gave us this profound and timeless bit of advice in Proverbs 4:5 . . . GET WISDOM!

This is advice that our modern world seems to overlook.

Enter the idea of **Quick Wisdom.**

The focus of **Quick Wisdom** is to help you and your friends be WISE!

237

Today, it seems to me that every young leader I meet wants wisdom, but needs it fast. We don't have the time with today's pace and pressures to go to a mountaintop and study ancient manuscripts in Sanskrit. Thus—"Quick Access to Timeless Wisdom." My focus: three to ten times times per month I plan to send "QuickWisdom" emails to pass on the very best "wisdom nuggets" I can give you each month to help strengthen you and your friends.

Free to you and your friends.

Quick Wisdom is one hundred percent free to you and your friends.

Fortunately, the email technology of today is such that you can enroll ten friends or one-hundred to receive the **Quick Wisdom** email. It takes me the same amount of time to send you an email as it does to send it to all of your protégés/friends. I want to use my unique exposure to great wisdom to strengthen you and your friends for a lifetime.

Thank you, my friend, for telling your friends about **Quick Wisdom**!

APPENDIX F

Speaking Topics/Bobb Biehl

Personal Development

Focusing Your Life

❑ **"Fog Cutting Arrow"**
Clarifying Any Topic Quickly ... Avoiding the Frustration of Mental Fog
❑ **"The NorthStar"**
Keeping a Clear Sense of Life Direction… Avoiding The "Lost At Sea" Feeling

Asking "Fog-Cutting" Questions

❑ **"The Dream Sparking Questions"**
Getting Your Thinking "Outside of the Box"…
Avoiding "Same ol' Same ol'" Results

Balancing Competing Priorities

❑ **"The Annual Balance Calendar"**
Balancing Your Life… Avoiding the Feeling of the Day to Day Busyness Drift

Communicating With Confidence

❑ **"The You Focus Model"**
Mastering "You Focus"… Avoiding "Egocentric" Communication

Organizational Development

Planning Your Organization's Future

❑ **"The "Team Focus Arrow" (50,000 Foot Level)**
Focusing Top Leadership's Thinking…Avoiding Team Confusion
❑ **"The Masterplanning Arrow" (20,000 Foot Level)**
Getting Your Team on the "Same Sheet of Music"…Reducing Team
Mis-Communication
❑ **"The Boulders Sheet" (Organizational Level)**
Keeping Your Team Focused on Boulders…Avoiding Team Drift and Stagnation

Building A "Championship" Team

❑ **"The Leadership Star"**
Upgrading Your Current Team…Avoiding "Bureaucratic" Thinking

Generating Consistent Cash Flow

❑ **"The Marketing Process"**
Generating Profit…Avoiding a "Warehouse Full of Unsold Inventory"

Managing Resources Wisely

❑ **"The 'Vital Signs' & 'Standards' of Healthy Growth"**
Projecting Your Team's 10-Year Future… Avoiding Dangerous Trends
(Blind Spots)

Please send me the following (free of charge):
- ❏ Masterplanning Group's tool catalogue
- ❏ Consulting information
- ❏ Speaking information

Name _____

Title _____

Organization _____

Address _____

City _____ State _____ Zip _____

Daytime telephone (_____) _____

Fax (_____) _____

E-Mail _____

Contact:
   Fax: (352) 385-2827
   Toll free fax: (888) 443-1976
   Ordering: (800) 443-1976
   Web: www.Aylen.com

Thank You!